# Welcome

BREATHE IN the pine-scented air, taste sugar cookies fresh from the oven, gaze at sparkling strings of lights...the holiday season is a time to savor. And you'll find over 150 new ways to do just that inside *Country Woman Christmas 2009*.

This special holiday treasury has everything you need for Yuletide celebrations, from delectable food and merry party ideas to dazzling home accents and handmade gifts.

Menu planning is easy with 105 never-before-published recipes, including scrumptious appetizers, entrees, cookies and more delights sure to become family favorites.

Deck the halls like never before with dozens of do-it-yourself Noel decorations, clever handcrafts and other creative how-tos filled with Christmas spirit.

Featuring heartfelt stories of miracles and touching poetry, too, *Country Woman Christmas 2009* will bring endless warmth, wonder and cheer to this holiday season—and many more to come!

54

12

22

# Country Woman
# *Christmas*
## 2009

## ON THE COVER
Santa's Workshop
Cupcakes, p. 76

---

### More Sparkle—All Year Long!
You don't have to wait until next Christmas to get more of the delightful recipes, crafts, decorations, stories and ideas featured in this book. They're in every issue of *Country Woman* magazine! To order for yourself or as a gift, visit *www.countrywomanmagazine.com* or call 1-800/344-6913.

**SENIOR VICE PRESIDENT, EDITOR IN CHIEF:**
Catherine Cassidy

**VICE PRESIDENT, EXECUTIVE EDITOR/BOOKS:**
Heidi Reuter Lloyd

**CREATIVE DIRECTOR:** Ardyth Cope

**FOOD DIRECTOR:** Diane Werner RD

**SENIOR EDITOR/BOOKS:** Mark Hagen

**EDITOR:** Michelle Bretl

**ASSOCIATE EDITOR:** Amy Glander

**CRAFT EDITOR:** Jane Craig

**ART DIRECTOR:** Gretchen Trautman

**CONTENT PRODUCTION SUPERVISOR:** Julie Wagner

**DESIGN LAYOUT ARTISTS:** Nancy Novak (lead),
Kathy Crawford, Catherine Fletcher

**PROOFREADER:** Linne Bruskewitz

**RECIPE ASSET SYSTEMS:** Coleen Martin,
Sue A. Jurack

**PREMEDIA SUPERVISOR:** Scott Berger

**RECIPE TESTING AND EDITING:**
Taste of Home Test Kitchen

**FOOD PHOTOGRAPHY:** Reiman Photo Studio

**GRAPHIC DESIGN ASSOCIATE:** Heather Miller

**EDITORIAL ASSISTANT:** Barb Czysz

**COVER PHOTO PHOTOGRAPHER:** Rob Hagen

**COVER FOOD STYLIST:** Jennifer Janz

**COVER SET STYLIST:** Jennifer Bradley Vent

**CHIEF MARKETING OFFICER:** Lisa Karpinski

**VICE PRESIDENT/BOOK MARKETING:** Dan Fink

**CREATIVE DIRECTOR/CREATIVE MARKETING:**
Jim Palmen

**The Reader's Digest Association, Inc.**

**PRESIDENT AND CHIEF EXECUTIVE OFFICER:**
Mary G. Berner

**PRESIDENT, FOOD & ENTERTAINING:**
Suzanne M. Grimes

**PRESIDENT, CONSUMER MARKETING:**
Dawn Zier

International Standard Book Number (10):
0-89821-629-X
International Standard Book Number (13):
978-0-89821-629-5
International Standard Serial Number:
1093-6750

*Timeless Recipes from Trusted Home Cooks*®
is a registered trademark of Reiman Media Group, Inc.

Printed in U.S.A.

For other Taste of Home books and products,
visit *ShopTasteofHome.com*.

## Share Your Holiday Joy

DO YOU celebrate Christmas in a special way? If so, we'd like to know! We're already gathering material for the next edition of *Country Woman Christmas*. And we need your help!

Does your family carry on a Yuletide tradition? Or do you deck your halls in some festive way? Maybe you know of a Christmas-loving country woman others might like to meet.

Do you have a nostalgic or inspirational story to share? Perhaps you've written holiday poetry or fiction.

We'd also like *original* Christmas quilt patterns and craft projects, plus handmade gifts, decorations, etc. And don't forget to include your best-loved recipes for holiday main courses, side dishes, appetizers, desserts, breads, cookies, candies, etc.

Send your ideas and photos to "CW Christmas Book," 5400 S. 60th Street, Greendale WI 53129. (Enclose a self-addressed stamped envelope if you'd like materials returned.) Or E-mail your ideas and photos to *bookeditors@reimanpub.com* (write "CW Christmas" on the subject line).

# Christmas Decorating

*Spread holiday cheer all through your house with the festive, do-it-yourself designs in this chapter.*

# Season's Greenery

*Want fresh ideas for florals? In this section, you'll find eye-catching arrangements you can easily make to spruce up your home.*

IT'S ONLY NATURAL to decorate for Christmas with pine boughs, poinsettias, sprigs of holly and other greenery. But if you're starting to tire of the same old wreath, centerpiece or swag, look here! We've featured delightfully different accents that branch out from the ordinary.

Need something to dress up an indoor railing? An empty bench…or maybe the front porch? From pretty cone-shaped containers to mini trees and a unique three-dimensional wreath, these December designs are sure to grow on you.

Each one is a simple-to-make project that takes mere moments to complete—no special skills or materials required. But the results are so impressive, your family and friends will never suspect they were handmade.

The hardest part of assembling these decorations? Trying to choose which kinds of Christmas florals and embellishments you want to use for your creations!

## Pretty Petite

This countrified little pine looks like a ready-made decoration purchased from the store. But you can create this accent yourself using a 12-inch piece of wired pine branch garland. Press the branches down to flatten the garland and cut it into a triangle shape to resemble a tree. Then decorate it with buttons, strips of fabric, pinecones or any trims you like.

# Homegrown Cones

With so many fun scrapbook papers available, why not bring some into your floral displays? In the photo at left, 12-inch square sheets of paper make lovely cone-shaped holders for artificial poinsettias. To make a cone, turn your paper wrong side up and mark the center of the bottom edge (this is where the cone's bottom point will be). Starting with the corner to the left of the mark, roll the paper into a cone—keeping the point at the marked spot—and tape the paper to secure it.

For smaller cones, simply buy the 8-inch squares of paper sold with other scrapbook papers…or cut any piece of paper into a square of whatever size you'd like. Need to reinforce a cone to hold heavier items? Make another same-size cone to slip inside, then trim the top edge of the inside cone so it's not visible above the outside one.

*(Continued on next page)*

# Carried Away

Just about any container that catches your eye at a flea market, yard sale or secondhand store can make a festive holiday accent when you fill it with florals. Here, a decorative metal can gets a Christmasy makeover thanks to faux evergreen boughs, berry clusters and fruits. Tie a simple ribbon bow to the handle for the perfect finish.

# Merry Mock-Ups

Go out on a limb with your outdoor decorating—hang up a cluster of these rustic little trees made of natural materials. *Country Woman* Craft Editor Jane Craig drilled holes into branches and pushed juniper twigs into the holes.

# Wreath Redo

This dimensional design puts a twice-as-nice twist on the usual wreath. Begin by wrapping pine garland around two large wooden embroidery hoops, completely covering them. Then carefully push one hoop halfway through the other, and presto—you have a fun sphere shape that can dangle from a shepherd's hook. Decorate the sphere with a faux cardinal, holly berries, a battery-operated candle and spray-on snow.

fresh Snowfall

# Words of Welcome

*Spell out your Christmas spirit this holiday season by decking the halls with festive words and phrases. You're sure to make a statement!*

IT'S A LETTER-PERFECT way of decorating—using your favorite words or phrases as expressive home accents. Not only does this idea suit just about any interior style, but it also gives you endless possibilities for Christmas.

In this section, we've highlighted six seasonal projects that display decorative letters. They're easy to create and can go everywhere from doorways and shelves to your fireplace mantel and dining table.

Hang up a "Ho Ho Ho" garland for a party...wrap napkins with "Joy" rings...add a "fresh snowfall" trim to a framed winter photo...each design is sure to delight your holiday guests.

Want suggestions to jump-start your imagination? Focus on common Christmastime words and expressions, such as Peace, Cheer, Noel, Joy, Season's Greetings, Yuletide, Faith, Hope and Believe.

To get more ideas, look at Christmas carols, stories or Bible passages. For example, consider song titles such as "O Holy Night," "Let It Snow" and "Jingle Bells." Or, use "The Night Before Christmas" and other lines from the famous poem "A Visit from St. Nicholas."

No matter where you look for inspiration, you'll send a message of glad tidings. So go ahead—express yourself!

## Letter Lineup

As a decoration for a Christmas party or all season long, a string of words makes a merry trim for hearths, entrances, railings and more. The ready-made, stiff felt letters shown in the photo at right were purchased from a craft store. You could also cut your own letters and punch holes for the cord.

## Defining Discs

Tuck your holiday DVDs, music CDs and photo discs into these cheery envelopes. Just cut one back and one front piece from paper and stitch them together using a sewing machine. Then add labels...or even Christmas greetings to create gifts.

## Caption Creativity

Enjoy scrapbooking or other paper crafts? Use those techniques to make the easy home accent at left. Simply create any seasonal scrapbook-style page you like and place it in a frame for display. In the example shown, a rub-on provides a "fresh snowfall" caption and snowflake details—the perfect finishing touches for a heartwarming winter photograph.

*(Continued on next page)*

# *Spelled Centerpiece*

Get your dinner conversation started with this festive foldout, made with chipboard panels from a lacing card kit (sold in craft stores). They're joined with ribbon and trimmed for Christmas with a variety of papers and embellishments.

# *Building Blocks*

Here's a fun (and versatile!) idea for small spaces. Associate Editor Amy Glander covered plain wood cubes with paper and letters, then rubbed the sanded edges with black ink. Choose words of any length and stack them as high as you like.

# Writing with Wire

Why buy pricey napkin rings at the store? You can serve up these elegant wire creations in a flash. All you need is a package of precut 14-gauge copper wire (available in assorted colors at craft stores). Using your fingers, carefully bend one wire piece to form a word and hook the ends in back. Rub the wire a bit with your fingers to warm it for easier bending.

# An Extreme Makeover Creates a
# *Farmhouse Full of Cheer*

*By Lori Arndt, Raymond, Wisconsin*

AS SOON as frost whitens the countryside, I'm ready to start decking my halls for Christmas...but not with the holiday decorations that typically fill retail stores.

Instead, I trim my home with Yuletide accents of a different sort: one-of-a-kind antique treasures, flea market finds and made-with-love handcrafts.

They perfectly reflect the character of my century-old farmhouse nestled along a country road in Raymond, Wisconsin—a farmhouse I restored from the brink of ruin with hard work and lots of tender loving care.

### City Girl Goes Country

As a girl growing up in rural Wisconsin, I longed for the excitement of big-city life. After college, I lived in town for many years. But the crowded urban scene grew old. Missing the country, I knew it was time for a change.

While I was considering my options, I heard that a family friend had bought foreclosed farmland not far from where I grew up. He'd sold off most of it but still had a parcel with a dilapidated farmhouse, which he hoped would appeal to buyers looking for a fixer-upper.

A fixer-upper, it was! Time had really taken its toll, and the 1910 house had fallen into severe disrepair. But with one look, I instantly fell in love—and wanted to bring it back to life.

So on my 29th birthday, I became the proud owner of this run-down but irresistible farmhouse.

### Rustic Restoration

My handy family members helped me transform this 100-year-old homestead into a modern dwelling. We replaced the plumbing, electrical system, roof, windows and siding. Plus, we rebuilt the entire kitchen and bathroom!

Despite these changes, I tried to retain the home's historic elements and restore them to their original condition.

My most treasured item is the antique china buffet, which first belonged to the dairy farmer who had lived on the property. Wanting to return the piece to its

*(Continued on next page)*

**ANTIQUES ENTHUSIAST** Lori Arndt (left) recruited the help of family members to bring her historic Raymond, Wisconsin farmhouse back to its original glory. The yearlong renovation project yielded an updated yet charming country home full of antique treasures, including the china buffet (far left) and chandelier (below) in the living room. Both are original to the 1910 farmhouse and make perfect display areas for decorations each Christmas.

**FLEA MARKET FINDS** abound in this restored rural dwelling. Lori's framed vintage Christmas cards (below) complement the original antiques and other Yuletide trimmings in the living room.

*Christmas Decorating* 🕊 **15**

this quaint homestead.

In our salvaging, we found *not*-so-desirable items as well. We had a good laugh when we came upon decades-old canning jars with unknown contents… and even a set of false teeth!

Then there was the most surprising discovery of all—six-foot-tall honeycombs hanging between the studs behind an old panel of siding. I actually had to call in a beekeeper to remove them. He later told me it was, to date, the best honey he'd ever tasted!

### There's No Place Like Home

I must admit that, at first, the prospect of living in a big, old farmhouse in a rural area spooked me a bit. But after all the hard work we put into the house and the small pieces of history we discovered along the way, I can't imagine any other place feeling more like home.

This is especially true at Christmastime, when I love to get creative and decorate my house for the season. Red and green florals, jars of homemade holiday jam, a handcrafted Father Christmas and a bell accented with holly are just a few of the ways I add some holiday magic to these old walls.

There's really nowhere I'd rather be on a winter's day than curled up on my cozy living-room chair, surrounded by my antique treasures and a scenic view of rolling, snow-covered hills. To me, life doesn't get much better!

home, I bid top-dollar for it an at estate sale. Now, at Christmas, I dress it up with Yuletide decorations such as poinsettias, framed vintage greeting cards and a knit stocking.

The chandelier is another authentic gem. After some rewiring and a thorough polish, my father hung it in its original spot in the living room. It's perfect for draping a green garland and strings of twinkling beads.

In the course of our renovation, we came upon many unexpected discoveries. Among them was an old door we affixed to the wall of the loft in the kitchen. The door adds a bit of mystery

to the loft, where I like to display decorative snowmen, miniature Christmas trees and other holiday decor.

A large porcelain sink, rustic doorknobs, a cement pond with a fountain in the backyard and other cherished items are still in place to reveal the history of

**BEFORE AND AFTER PHOTOS** (above and top) show the extreme makeover Lori Arndt gave her turn-of-the-century farmhouse. The loft above the kitchen (below), a new addition to the house that features an original door, serves as an overhead display area for Christmas figurines and greenery.

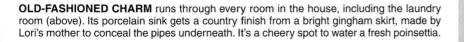

**OLD-FASHIONED CHARM** runs through every room in the house, including the laundry room (above). Its porcelain sink gets a country finish from a bright gingham skirt, made by Lori's mother to conceal the pipes underneath. It's a cheery spot to water a fresh poinsettia.

**HANDCRAFTED ACCENTS** bring a warmth that only they can bring to the many nooks and crannies of a farmhouse. Among the Yuletide decorations created by Lori's mother, a folksy Father Christmas (right) stands proudly near the antique china buffet in the living room, welcoming visitors during December.

**SMALL TREASURES** add up to make big spaces cozy. On one of the farmhouse's original doorknobs, a rustic bell (left) trimmed with plaid ribbon, faux berries and greenery suits the old-time style while ringing in the holiday season.

# A Thrifty Christmas

*Why spend sackfuls of money on holiday decor? Transform ordinary household items and leftover craft supplies into inexpensive but elegant accents.*

DO YOU have scraps of fabric stashed away in a sewing room? Stacks of old Christmas cards, waiting to be used for…something? Maybe your kitchen cupboard contains a no-longer-needed baking sheet, or your closet holds excess ornaments you just don't have room for on the tree.

Instead of leaving leftover items to take up valuable storage space—or tossing them in trash—check out the ideas here. You'll see clever ways of turning odds and ends into beautiful holiday decorations you can enjoy year after year.

Each delightful design is simple enough for just about anyone to create. And because they make use of on-hand objects, you won't have to empty your wallet in order to deck the house with festive accents.

Don't know what to do with extra compact discs? You'll be amazed at how those ordinary metallic circles can add glitter to your dining room table. Stuck with short lengths of ribbon at the end of the spool? Use them to embellish a miniature Christmas tree by assembling a set of super-quick but gorgeous ornaments.

Once you see all of the cheery but easy holiday trims you can create using scraps, you may just find yourself asking friends and family members for theirs, too!

## Compact Disc Dazzle

Here's a tasteful idea for unwanted compact discs: Put them on your dinner table! In the photo at right, a CD makes the perfect shiny, metallic base for a basic ball ornament. Attach a coordinating name card to the top of the ornament, and presto—you have a shimmering place marker for guests.

## Pretty Paperwork

Want to make use of old greeting cards or paper scraps? Cut out tag shapes (freehand or using a punch or die-cut machine), add ribbon and tie them around plain candle holders for a quick accent. Create extra tags to use on Christmas gifts!

## Outside the Box

If your leftover fabrics are piling up, turn your favorites into a pretty stack of presents using three papier-mache boxes of different sizes. Brush the sides of each box with decoupage medium and wrap that section with a wide strip of fabric. Fold the fabric edges to the bottom and inside the box, securing them with adhesive. Use the same technique to cover the lid.

*(Continued on next page)*

# Fresh from the Oven

With paper craft supplies, you can turn a worn cookie sheet into a fun December calendar for the kitchen. Make the year removeable and attach the dates with magnets so they can be shifted—you'll have a calendar you can use year after year!

# Branching Out

If your tree is overcrowded with ornaments, take off the extras and try this idea from Wendy Borchert of Whitefish Bay, Wisconsin. She packed them inside purchased wire gift boxes and added strings of lights, creating eye-catching accents.

# Ribbon Rescue

What to do with those short snippets left on your spools of ribbon? Stuff them inside clear ball ornaments from the craft store. The pretty swirls of velvet, satin, grosgrain or other ribbon appear as though they're suspended in air, creating a delightful effect. If you like, combine different colors/prints…or add other embellishments.

# Gather Girlfriends for an
# After-Shopping Party!

Hit your favorite stores together, then enjoy a casual party afterward with delicious appetizers, beverages and a purse-shaped cake.

WHETHER you like to go Christmas shopping the day after Thanksgiving or closer to December 25, why not make a fun-filled day of it? Invite friends to join you for a group outing, then make the last stop your place for some great food, relaxation and plenty of holiday cheer.

In this section, we've featured an "After-Shopping Party" menu (pages 25-27) of scrumptious appetizers and beverages your friends will love. Each recipe can either be made ahead of time or whipped up in a just a few minutes on the day of your party. You'll even find a stylish purse-shaped cake—the perfect way to top off a day of shopping!

Plan on snapping pictures? We've also included directions for making a cute purse photo frame you can give each guest as a take-home memento. (Find this project on page 24.)

So go ahead—make your Christmas shopping day a memorable event with the ideas here. You'll have fun in the bag!

AT THE END of your fun-filled shopping day, give girl-friends the perfect memento—a purse picture frame displaying a snapshot from the event. (If you print digital photos at home, print your pictures during the party and fill the frames before the guests leave!)

These "handbags" are papier-mache frames, complete with beaded handles and available in craft stores. You can dress up the plain purses any way you like.

Sandy Rollinger of Apollo, Pennsylvania decorated the frames shown above by sponge-painting them with white and then two different shades of the same color (green or blue). She used a dauber to give the green purse white polka dots.

To finish, Sandy trimmed around the photo openings by gluing on rhinestones and beads. It's that simple...so you'll be able to make one for each guest in no time!

HERE'S AN EXTRA IDEA for the fun purse party favors at left! Each one has a clasp on top and opens up just like a regular purse. For an added treat, pop a little extra "something" into each handbag for guests to take with them. For example, include wrapped candies or extra photos.

## Purse Cake

~*Michelle Menjoulet, Murphy, Texas*

    1 package (18-1/4 ounces) white cake mix
    2 eggs
1-1/3 cups water
FROSTING:
   3/4 cup shortening
   3/4 cup butter, softened
     6 cups confectioners' sugar
   1/4 cup milk
1-1/2 teaspoons clear vanilla extract
Paste food coloring of your choice
Dragees
    1 piece wired ribbon (10 inches)
    1 plastic drinking straw, cut into 3-inch pieces

**1.** In a large bowl, combine the cake mix, eggs and water; beat on low speed for 30 seconds. Beat on medium for 2 minutes. Pour 4 cups batter into a greased and waxed paper-lined 9-in. square baking pan (discard remaining batter).

**2.** Bake at 350° for 30-35 minutes or until a toothpick inserted near the center comes out clean. Cool for 10 minutes before removing from pan to a wire rack to cool completely.

**3.** For frosting, in a large bowl, beat shortening and butter until light and fluffy. Add the confectioners' sugar, milk and vanilla; beat until smooth. Tint frosting as desired.

**4.** Using a serrated knife, level top of cake if necessary. Using dental floss, cut cake in half diagonally by starting at a top edge and pulling floss through to opposite bottom edge. Place cut sides of cakes together with wide ends at bottom; cut off top 3 in. Spread frosting between layers.

**5.** Transfer cake to a serving platter; spread frosting over the top and sides of cake. Decorate as desired with remaining frosting and dragees. For handle, insert each end of ribbon into a drinking straw piece; insert each end into top of cake. Store in the refrigerator. **Yield:** 9 servings.

## Party Menu

Cranberry Hot Toddies (p. 25)
Purse Cake (p. 25)
Tomato-Walnut Pesto Spread (p. 26)
Veggie Quiche Bundles (p. 26)
Beef Triangles & Chutney Dip (p. 26)
Apricot Brie (p. 27)
Chunky Corn Dip (p. 27)
Easy Bagel Dip (p. 27)
Sangria Wine (p. 27)

## Cranberry Hot Toddies

~*Sharon Delaney-Chronis, South Milwaukee, Wisconsin*

   2 cups unsweetened pineapple juice
   2 cups water
   1 can (16 ounces) jellied cranberry sauce
1/3 cup packed brown sugar
1/4 teaspoon ground cinnamon
1/4 teaspoon ground allspice
1/8 teaspoon ground cloves
1/8 teaspoon ground nutmeg
1/8 teaspoon salt
   2 tablespoons butter, cut into six pieces

In a large saucepan, combine the first nine ingredients. Bring to a boil. Reduce heat; cover and simmer for 1 hour, stirring occasionally. Serve in mugs; top with butter. **Yield:** 6 servings.

*Purse Cake*

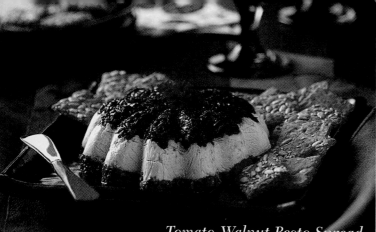

*Tomato-Walnut Pesto Spread*

# Tomato-Walnut Pesto Spread

*~Marsha Dawson, Appleton, Wisconsin*

>      3 tablespoons chopped patted dry oil-packed
>          sun-dried tomatoes
>      1 package (8 ounces) cream cheese, softened
>      1/2 cup grated Parmesan cheese
>      1/4 cup sour cream
>      2 tablespoons butter, softened
>      1/2 cup finely chopped walnuts
>      1/2 cup prepared pesto
> Assorted crackers

**1.** Line a 4-cup mold with plastic wrap; coat with cooking spray. Place tomatoes in bottom of mold; set aside.

**2.** In a large bowl, beat the cheeses, sour cream and butter until blended. In another bowl, combine walnuts and pesto. Spread cheese mixture over tomatoes in prepared mold; top with walnut mixture.

**3.** Bring edges of plastic wrap together over pesto; press down gently to seal. Refrigerate for at least 4 hours or until firm. Open plastic wrap; invert mold onto a serving plate. Serve with crackers. **Yield:** 2-1/3 cups.

# Veggie Quiche Bundles

*~Lorraine Caland, Thunder Bay, Ontario*

>      1 cup chopped fresh mushrooms
>      1/2 cup diced zucchini
>      1/4 cup chopped red onion
>      1 tablespoon plus 1/3 cup butter, *divided*
>      1 plum tomato, seeded and diced
>      3 eggs
>      1/2 cup milk
>      1 tablespoon prepared pesto
>      1/4 teaspoon coarsely ground pepper
>      1/2 cup crumbled feta cheese
>      1/2 cup shredded part-skim mozzarella cheese
>      12 sheets phyllo dough (14 inches x 9 inches)

**1.** In a small skillet, saute the mushrooms, zucchini and onion in 1 tablespoon butter until mushrooms are tender; stir in the tomato. In a small bowl, whisk the eggs, milk, pesto and pepper. In another bowl, combine the cheeses.

**2.** Melt the remaining butter. Place one sheet of phyllo dough on a work surface; brush with butter. Top with another sheet of phyllo; brush with butter. Repeat. Cut phyllo in half widthwise, then cut in half lengthwise.

**3.** Repeat with remaining phyllo dough and butter. Carefully place each stack in a greased muffin cup. Fill each with 4 teaspoons vegetable mixture, 1 tablespoon cheese mixture and 4 teaspoons egg mixture. Pinch corners of phyllo together and twist to seal.

**4.** Bake at 325° for 20-25 minutes or until golden brown. Serve warm. Refrigerate leftovers. **Yield:** 1 dozen.

# Beef Triangles & Chutney Dip

*~Carla DeVelder, Mishawaka, Indiana*

>      1 pound ground beef
>      1 small onion, finely chopped
>      1/3 cup dried currants
>      1/2 teaspoon salt
>      1/2 teaspoon ground cumin
>      1/4 teaspoon ground cinnamon
>      1/4 teaspoon ground nutmeg
>      1/8 teaspoon cayenne pepper
>      1/8 teaspoon pepper
>      1 tablespoon cornstarch
>      1/2 cup water
>      28 sheets phyllo dough (14 inches x 9 inches)
> Butter-flavored cooking spray
>      1/2 cup plain yogurt
>      1/2 cup chutney

**1.** In a large skillet, cook beef and onion over medium heat until meat is no longer pink; drain. Stir in currants and seasonings. Combine cornstarch and water until smooth; gradually stir into beef mixture. Bring to a boil; cook and stir for 2 minutes or until thickened. Remove from the heat.

**2.** Place one sheet of phyllo dough on a work surface with a short end facing you; spray sheet with butter-flavored spray. Place another sheet of phyllo on top and spritz with spray. (Keep remaining phyllo covered with plastic wrap to prevent it from drying out.) Cut the two layered sheets into four 14-in. x 2-1/4-in. strips.

**3.** Place a rounded teaspoonful of filling on lower corner of each strip. Fold dough over filling, forming a triangle. Fold

*Veggie Quiche Bundles*

*Apricot Brie*

triangle up, then fold triangle over, forming another triangle. Continue folding, like a flag, until you come to the end of the strip. Spritz end of dough with spray and press onto triangle to seal. Turn triangle and spritz top with spray. Repeat with remaining phyllo and filling.

**4.** Place triangles on baking sheets coated with cooking spray. Bake at 400° for 8-10 minutes or until golden brown. Combine yogurt and chutney. Serve with warm appetizers. **Yield:** 56 appetizers (1 cup sauce).

# Apricot Brie

~*Alice Goggin, Trabuco Canyon, California*

> 1/2 cup apricot preserves
> 1 tablespoon grated orange peel
> 1 tablespoon lemon juice
> 1 tablespoon orange juice
> 1/8 teaspoon ground cinnamon
> 1 round (8 ounces) **Brie** *or* **Camembert cheese**
Sliced French bread

In a small microwave-safe bowl, combine the first five ingredients. Cook, uncovered, on high for 1 minute or until heated through. Pour into a shallow 3-cup microwave-safe serving dish. Place cheese on preserve mixture. Cook 1 to 1-1/2 minutes longer or until cheese is softened. Serve with bread. **Yield:** 8 servings.

**Editor's Note:** This recipe was tested in a 1,100-watt microwave.

# Chunky Corn Dip

~*Pat Stevens, Granbury, Texas*

> 1 package (8 ounces) cream cheese, softened
> 1-1/2 cups mayonnaise
> 3 teaspoons ground cumin
> 2 cans (15-3/4 ounces *each*) whole kernel corn, drained
> 3/4 cup chopped green onions
> 1 can (4-1/4 ounces) chopped ripe olives
> 3 jalapeno peppers, seeded and chopped
Tortilla chip scoops

In a large bowl, beat the cream cheese, mayonnaise and cumin. Stir in the corn, onions, olives and jalapenos. Cover and refrigerate for at least 2 hours. Serve with tortilla chips. **Yield:** 5 cups.

**Editor's Note:** When cutting hot peppers, disposable gloves are recommended. Avoid touching your face.

# Easy Bagel Dip

~*Mary Merkwan, Wagner, South Dakota*

> 2 cups (16 ounces) sour cream
> 1-1/2 cups mayonnaise
> 2 tablespoons dried parsley flakes
> 2 tablespoons minced chives
> 2 teaspoons dill weed
> 1/4 teaspoon garlic salt
> 1 medium onion, finely chopped
> 2 packages (2-1/2 ounces *each*) thinly sliced dried beef, chopped
Plain bagels, split and cut into bite-size pieces

In a large bowl, combine sour cream and mayonnaise. Add the parsley, chives, dill and garlic salt. Stir in onion and dried beef. Cover and refrigerate dip overnight. Serve with bagels. **Yield:** 4-1/4 cups.

# Sangria Wine

~*Colleen Sturma, Milwaukee, Wisconsin*

> 1 bottle (750 milliliters) dry red wine
> 1 cup lemon-flavored rum
> 2 cans (12 ounces *each*) lemon-lime soda, chilled
> 2 medium lemons, sliced
> 2 medium limes, sliced
Ice cubes

In a large pitcher, combine the wine, rum and soda; add lemon and lime slices. Serve over ice. **Yield:** 10 servings.

*Sangria Wine*

# Holiday Recipes

For the scrumptious Christmas delights your family will love, look no further than this tasteful chapter.

Cranberry Coffee Cake

# Bountiful Brunch

*Christmas morning will shine even brighter when you treat loved ones to these golden pancakes, savory breakfast bakes and much more.*

## Cranberry Coffee Cake

*This sugar-dusted cake has tangy cranberry flavor and a nice crunch from walnuts. It's also a great take-along item because it's easily portable.* ~Lisa Williams, Steamboat Springs, Colorado

        1 cup butter, softened
        1 cup sugar
        2 eggs
        1 cup (8 ounces) sour cream
        1 teaspoon vanilla extract
        2 cups all-purpose flour
 1-1/2 teaspoons baking powder
    1/2 teaspoon baking soda
    1/2 teaspoon salt
        1 cup chopped walnuts
    1/2 cup whole-berry cranberry sauce
        1 teaspoon grated orange peel
        1 teaspoon ground cinnamon
        1 tablespoon confectioners' sugar

**1.** In a large bowl, cream butter and sugar until light and fluffy. Add eggs, one at a time, beating well after each addition. Stir in sour cream and vanilla. Combine the flour, baking powder, baking soda and salt. Gradually add to the creamed mixture.

**2.** Pour half of the batter into a greased and floured 10-in. fluted tube pan. In a small bowl, combine the walnuts, cranberry sauce, orange peel and cinnamon; spoon over batter. Top with remaining batter. Bake at 350° for 40-45 minutes or until a toothpick inserted near the center comes out clean.

**3.** Cool for 15 minutes before removing from pan to a wire rack to cool completely. Sprinkle with confectioners' sugar. **Yield:** 12 servings.

## Caramel Rolls

*You're sure to satisfy sweet tooths when you bake a pan of these ooey-gooey treats. They're best fresh from the oven after a few minutes of cooling.* ~Dawn Fagerstrom, Warren, Minnesota

        3 packages (7-1/2 ounces *each*) refrigerated
            buttermilk biscuits
    1/2 cup sugar
    1/2 teaspoon ground cinnamon
TOPPING:
    1/2 cup butter, cubed
    1/2 cup sugar
    1/2 cup packed brown sugar
    1/2 cup vanilla ice cream

**1.** Cut each biscuit into four pieces. Combine sugar and cinnamon. Roll each biscuit piece in cinnamon-sugar. Place in a greased 13-in. x 9-in. baking pan. In a small saucepan, combine the topping ingredients; cook and stir over medium heat until ice cream is melted and brown sugar is dissolved. Pour over the biscuits.

**2.** Bake at 350° for 25-30 minutes or until golden brown. Cool for 5 minutes before inverting onto a wire rack. Serve immediately. **Yield:** 12 servings.

## Orange Date Spread

*Dress up your bread, bagels and muffins for the holidays with a dollop of this delightful cream-cheese topping. You'll want to whip up an extra batch for hectic mornings on weekdays, too.* ~Veronica Johnson, Jefferson City, Missouri

    1/2 cup cream cheese, softened
    1/4 cup finely chopped dates
        1 tablespoon orange juice
    1/2 teaspoon grated orange peel
    1/8 teaspoon ground allspice
Assorted breads

In a small bowl, combine the first five ingredients. Serve with bread slices. **Yield:** 3/4 cup.

*Orange Date Spread*

*Pumpkin Pancakes with Apple Cider Compote*

3. Pour batter by 1/4 cupfuls onto a hot griddle; flatten with the back of a spoon. Turn when the undersides are browned; cook until the second sides are golden brown. Serve with compote and remaining pecans. Store leftover compote in the refrigerator. **Yield:** 14 pancakes (5 cups compote).

**Editor's Note:** Leftover compote may be served with hot cereal or ice cream. It's also a tasty condiment for pork chops.

# Ham & Swiss Bread Pudding

*Here's a hearty brunch item loaded with ham, Swiss cheese and cream, plus layers of sliced French bread. It's great for any special occasion.* ~Kelly Williams, Morganville, New Jersey

   1/4 cup plus 3 tablespoons butter, melted, *divided*
    18 slices day-old French bread (3/4 inch thick), *divided*
   1/2 cup whole grain mustard
1-1/2 cups cubed fully cooked ham
     1 cup sliced fresh mushrooms
     2 garlic cloves, minced
   1/4 cup chopped green onions
     2 cups (8 ounces) shredded Swiss cheese
     8 eggs
     4 cups heavy whipping cream
   1/2 teaspoon salt
   1/2 teaspoon pepper
     2 tablespoons minced fresh parsley
Warm maple syrup, optional

1. Pour 1/4 cup butter into a 13-in. x 9-in. baking dish; set aside. Spread both sides of bread with mustard. Arrange nine slices in baking dish.

2. In a large skillet, saute the ham, mushrooms and garlic in remaining butter until mushrooms are tender. Add the onions; cook 1 minute longer or until onions are crisp-tender. Spoon over bread; sprinkle with cheese. Arrange remaining bread on top. In a large bowl, beat the eggs, cream, salt and pepper. Stir in parsley; pour over bread.

3. Place dish in a larger baking pan. Fill larger pan with hot water to a depth of 1 in. Bake at 325° for 50-60 minutes or until a knife inserted near the center comes out clean. Let stand for 5 minutes before serving. Drizzle with maple syrup if desired. **Yield:** 9 servings.

# Pumpkin Pancakes with Apple Cider Compote

*Try these spiced cakes for an out-of-the-ordinary breakfast. The syrup made from pie filling is the crowning touch on these lip-smacking delights.* ~Margie Mitchell, Portland, Oregon

     1 cup sugar
     2 tablespoons cornstarch
   1/2 teaspoon ground cinnamon
     2 cups apple cider *or* juice
     2 tablespoons orange juice
     1 can (21 ounces) apple pie filling
     2 tablespoons butter
PANCAKES:
     1 cup old-fashioned oats
1-1/4 cups all-purpose flour
     2 tablespoons brown sugar
     2 teaspoons baking powder
     1 teaspoon pumpkin pie spice
     1 teaspoon ground cinnamon
   1/4 teaspoon salt
     1 egg
1-1/2 cups milk
     1 cup canned pumpkin
     3 tablespoons maple syrup
     2 tablespoons canola oil
     1 cup chopped pecans, toasted, *divided*

1. In a large saucepan, combine sugar, cornstarch and cinnamon. Stir in cider and orange juice until smooth. Bring to a boil; cook and stir for 2 minutes or until thickened. Stir in pie filling and butter. Remove from heat; set aside and keep warm.

2. For pancakes, place oats in a food processor; cover and process until ground. Transfer to a large bowl; add the flour, brown sugar, baking powder, pie spice, cinnamon and salt. In another bowl, whisk the egg, milk, pumpkin, syrup and oil. Stir into dry ingredients just until moistened; fold in 1/2 cup chopped pecans.

# Strawberry Banana Spritzer

(Pictured on page 33)

*This refreshing beverage is a snap to prepare. The bananas and strawberries can be blended in advance and frozen, saving time if you're serving a large group. It's also fun to experiment with different fruit combinations.* ~Karen Ann Bland, Gove, Texas

     6 cups orange juice
     2 containers (10 ounces *each*) frozen sweetened sliced strawberries, partially thawed
     2 medium ripe bananas, cut into chunks
     3 cups club soda

In a blender, combine the orange juice, strawberries and bananas in batches until smooth. Transfer to a large pitcher. Refrigerate until serving. Just before serving, add club soda. **Yield:** 12 servings (3 quarts).

## Anise Fruit Bowl

(Pictured on page 33)

*With eight kinds of fruit, this eye-opening salad has become a family favorite for breakfast. You could even serve the tangy medley alongside a slice of cake and add whipped cream for a luscious dessert.* ~Juanita Stone, Graham, North Carolina

    2 cups water
1-1/2 cups sugar
    3 tablespoons lemon juice
    2 tablespoons aniseed
1/2 teaspoon salt
    1 fresh pineapple, peeled and cubed
    1 small cantaloupe, peeled, seeded and cubed
1/2 pound seedless red grapes
    2 large bananas, sliced
    2 medium nectarines, sliced
    2 medium oranges, peeled and sectioned
    2 medium kiwifruit, peeled and sliced
    1 large pink grapefruit, peeled and sectioned

**1.** In a large saucepan, bring the water, sugar, lemon juice, aniseed and salt to a boil. Reduce heat; simmer for 10-15 minutes or until slightly thickened. Cool slightly; cover and refrigerate until chilled.

**2.** In a large bowl, combine the remaining ingredients. Pour syrup over fruit; toss to coat. Refrigerate until serving. Serve with a slotted spoon. **Yield:** 18 servings (3/4 cup).

## Golden Danish Twists

*These tender twists have a rich cream cheese filling and sweet, lemony icing. My family likes them for breakfast after opening Christmas gifts.* ~Annie De La Hoz, Delta, Colorado

    2 packages (1/4 ounce *each*) active dry yeast
1/2 cup warm water (110° to 115°)
    1 cup warm milk (110° to 115°)
    1 cup canned pumpkin
    2 eggs
1/4 cup sugar
1/4 cup butter, softened
    3 teaspoons salt
    6 to 6-1/2 cups all-purpose flour
FILLING:
    2 packages (8 ounces *each*) cream cheese, softened
1/3 cup confectioners' sugar
1/2 cup heavy whipping cream
    2 teaspoons grated lemon peel
    1 teaspoon vanilla extract
ICING:
1/4 cup butter, cubed
    2 tablespoons all-purpose flour
1/4 cup lemon juice

2-2/3 cups confectioners' sugar
    1 tablespoon grated lemon peel
3/4 cup sliced almonds

**1.** In a large bowl, dissolve yeast in warm water. Add the milk, pumpkin, eggs, sugar, butter, salt and 3 cups flour; beat until smooth. Stir in enough remaining flour to make a soft dough.

**2.** Turn onto a floured surface; knead until smooth and elastic, about 6-8 minutes. Place in a greased bowl, turning once to grease top. Cover and let rise in a warm place until doubled, about 1 hour.

**3.** Meanwhile, for filling, in a small bowl, beat cream cheese and confectioners' sugar until smooth. Beat in the cream, lemon peel and vanilla.

**4.** Punch dough down; transfer to a lightly floured surface. Divide dough in half. Roll one portion into an 18-in. x 12-in. rectangle. Spread half of the filling lengthwise over half of the dough to within 1/2 in. of edges. Fold dough over filling; seal edges. Cut into 18 strips. Twist and loosely coil each strip. Tuck end under; pinch to seal. Place on greased baking sheets. Repeat with remaining dough and filling.

**5.** Cover and let rise until doubled, about 30 minutes. Bake at 375° for 12-15 minutes or until twists are golden brown. Remove to wire racks.

**6.** For icing, in a small saucepan, melt butter. Stir in flour until smooth. Stir in juice. Bring to a boil; cook and stir for 2 minutes or until thickened. Remove from the heat. Stir in confectioners' sugar and lemon peel until blended. Drizzle over warm twists. Sprinkle with almonds. Refrigerate leftovers. **Yield:** 3 dozen.

*Golden Danish Twists*

# Bacon Cheese Swirls

*With a creamy filling, these little bites are real crowd-pleasers. They're so easy to make using refrigerated dough and just five other ingredients.* ~Karen Grant, Tulare, California

   1 tube (8 ounces) refrigerated crescent rolls
   2 packages (3 ounces *each*) cream cheese, softened
   5 bacon strips, cooked and crumbled
   2 tablespoons finely chopped onion
   1 teaspoon milk
 2/3 cup shredded Parmesan cheese

**1.** Separate dough into four 8-in. x 6-in. rectangles; gently press perforations to seal. In a small bowl, combine the cream cheese, bacon, onion and milk. Spread evenly over rectangles.

**2.** Roll up jelly-roll style, starting with a long side; pinch seams to seal. Cut each roll into eight slices; place cut side down on ungreased baking sheets.

**3.** Bake at 375° for 7 minutes. Sprinkle with Parmesan cheese. Bake 5-8 minutes longer or until golden brown. Serve appetizers warm or at room temperature. Refrigerate leftovers. **Yield:** 32 appetizers.

# Smoked Salmon And Egg Wraps

*These cheesy breakfast wraps are terrific when you're serving a crowd. The flavor of the salmon comes through with a hint of dill from the eggs.* ~Mary Lou Wayman, Salt Lake City, Utah

Smoked Salmon and Egg Wraps

  12 eggs
 1/4 cup snipped fresh dill *or* 4 teaspoons dill weed
   2 tablespoons milk
 1/2 teaspoon seasoned salt
  10 flour tortillas (8 inches)
   1 package (4 ounces) smoked cooked salmon
 1/2 cup finely chopped red onion
   6 ounces Havarti cheese, thinly sliced

**1.** In a large bowl, whisk the eggs, dill, milk and seasoned salt. Coat a large nonstick skillet with cooking spray and place over medium heat. Add egg mixture. Cook and stir over medium heat until eggs are completely set.

**2.** Spoon a scant 1/3 cup egg mixture down the center of each tortilla. Top with salmon, onion and cheese. Fold opposite sides of tortilla over filling (sides will not meet in center). Roll up tortilla, beginning at one of the open ends. Place the wraps, seam side down, in a 15-in. x 10-in. baking pan coated with cooking spray.

**3.** Cover and bake at 350° for 10 minutes or until cheese is melted. **Yield:** 10 servings.

# Italian Tomato Tart

*Give your Christmas brunch a taste of old-world Italy with this hearty deep-dish tart. The breakfast pie is fresh-tasting and has a tender filling.* ~Jeanne Tongson, South Beloit, Illinois

    1 sheet refrigerated pie pastry
1-1/2 cups (6 ounces) shredded part-skim mozzarella
       cheese, *divided*
    1 pound bulk Italian sausage
    1 small onion, chopped
  1/2 cup finely chopped green pepper
    4 garlic cloves, minced
    6 plum tomatoes, seeded and cut into wedges
  3/4 cup loosely packed basil leaves, chopped
  1/2 cup mayonnaise
  1/4 cup grated Parmigiano-Reggiano cheese
    2 tablespoons minced fresh parsley
  1/8 teaspoon white pepper

**1.** Line a 9-in. deep-dish pie plate with pastry. Trim pastry to 1/2 in. beyond edge of plate; flute edges. Line unpricked pastry with a double thickness of heavy-duty foil. Bake at 450° for 8 minutes. Remove foil; bake 5 minutes longer. Remove to a wire rack; sprinkle with 1/2 cup mozzarella cheese. Reduce heat to 375°.

**2.** In a large skillet, cook the sausage, onion, green pepper and garlic over medium heat until meat is no longer pink; drain. Spoon sausage mixture into shell.

**3.** Arrange tomatoes over sausage mixture. In a small bowl, combine basil, mayonnaise, Parmigiano-Reggiano, parsley, pepper and remaining mozzarella; spoon over tomatoes.

**4.** Bake at 375° for 20-25 minutes or until a knife inserted near the center comes out clean. Let stand for 10 minutes before cutting. **Yield:** 8 servings.

*Strawberry Banana Spritzer (p. 30)*
*Anise Fruit Bowl (p. 31)*
*Italian Tomato Tart*
*Bacon Cheese Swirls*

Swirled Herb Bread

# Fresh-Baked Breads

## Swirled Herb Bread

*The spiral filling lends fantastic flavor to this big, even-textured loaf. It's a great complement to a spaghetti or lasagna dinner. For an added touch, sprinkle some Parmesan cheese on top.*
~Kari Boncher, Green Bay, Wisconsin

    5 to 6 cups all-purpose flour
    2 packages (1/4 ounce *each*) active dry yeast
1-1/2 teaspoons salt
    1 teaspoon sugar
    1 cup milk
    3/4 cup water
    1/2 cup butter, cubed
FILLING:
    1/2 cup butter, softened
    2 teaspoons dried basil
    2 teaspoons dill weed
    1 teaspoon dried minced onion
    1 teaspoon garlic powder

**1.** In a large bowl, combine 3 cups flour, yeast, salt and sugar. In a saucepan, heat the milk, water and butter to 120°-130°. Add to the dry ingredients; beat until smooth. Stir in enough remaining flour to form a soft dough (the dough will be sticky).

**2.** Turn onto a floured surface; knead until smooth and elastic, about 6-8 minutes. Place in a greased bowl, turning once to grease the top. Cover and let rise in a warm place until doubled, about 1 hour. Meanwhile, in a small bowl, combine filling ingredients; set aside.

**3.** Punch down dough; divide in half. Turn onto a lightly floured surface. Roll each portion into a 12-in. x 8-in. rectangle. Spread filling over each to within 1/2 in. of edges. Roll up jelly-roll style, starting with a short side; pinch seams to seal and tuck ends under. Place seam side down in two greased 8-in. x 4-in. loaf pans.

**4.** Cover and let rise in a warm place until doubled, about 30 minutes. Bake at 375° for 35-40 minutes or until browned. Cool for 10 minutes before removing from pans to wire racks. **Yield:** 2 loaves (12 slices each).

## Lemon Carrot Bread

*Lemon and carrot may seem like an unusual combination, but the result is a quick bread that really tastes terrific. I know this recipe is a winner because I bring a loaf to our annual church festival every year, and I always get requests to bake it again.*
~Hazel Schultz, Painesville, Ohio

    3/4 cup butter, softened
1-1/2 cups sugar
    3 eggs
    1 tablespoon lemon juice
2-1/4 cups all-purpose flour
    2 teaspoons baking powder
    1/2 teaspoon baking soda
    1/4 teaspoon salt
    1/2 cup milk
    1 cup shredded carrots
    3/4 cup chopped pecans
    2 tablespoons grated lemon peel

**1.** In a large bowl, cream butter and sugar until light and fluffy. Add eggs, one at a time, beating well after each addition. Stir in lemon juice. Combine the flour, baking powder, baking soda and salt; add to the creamed mixture alternately with milk. Stir in the carrots, pecans and lemon peel.

**2.** Transfer to two greased 8-in. x 4-in. loaf pans. Bake at 350° for 40-45 minutes or until a toothpick inserted near the center comes out clean. Cool for 10 minutes before removing from pans to wire racks. **Yield:** 2 loaves (12 slices each).

*Lemon Carrot Bread*

# Lemon Tea Biscuits

*These flaky, from-scratch goodies have a subtle but pleasant tang that comes from both the lemon juice in the dough and the accompanying lemon butter. Serve these biscuits the next time you host a holiday tea party for friends, family or co-workers.*
*~Jane Rossen, Binghamton, New York*

   4 cups all-purpose flour
   1/4 cup sugar
 1-1/2 teaspoons baking soda
   1 teaspoon salt
   2/3 cup shortening
   1 cup milk
   6 tablespoons lemon juice
LEMON BUTTER:
   1/2 cup butter, softened
 4-1/2 teaspoons lemon juice
   2 teaspoons grated lemon peel
   1 tablespoon finely chopped onion, optional

**1.** In a large bowl, combine the flour, sugar, baking soda and salt. Cut in the shortening until the mixture resembles fine crumbs. Stir in the milk and lemon juice just until moistened. Turn the dough onto a lightly floured surface; knead dough 8-10 times.

**2.** Roll out to 1/2-in. thickness; cut with a floured 2-1/2-in. biscuit cutter. Place 2 in. apart on ungreased baking sheets. Bake at 450° for 8-10 minutes or until golden brown.

**3.** Meanwhile, in a small bowl, combine lemon-butter ingredients until blended. Serve with warm biscuits. **Yield:** 16 biscuits (1/2 cup butter).

*Lemon Tea Biscuits*

# Mushroom Ricotta Bread

*The texture of this bread is so wonderfully soft, it seems to melt in your mouth! Garlic adds some zip, and the ricotta cheese lends richness.* *~Aimee Rubenstein, Roswell, Georgia*

   2 packages (1/4 ounce *each*) active dry yeast
   2/3 cup warm water (110° to 115°)
   4 to 5 cups all-purpose flour
   1 cup whole wheat flour
   1/3 cup packed brown sugar
   1/3 cup olive oil
   1 egg
   1 teaspoon salt
FILLING:
   1/2 cup chopped fresh mushrooms
   4 garlic cloves, minced
   1 tablespoon butter
   1/2 cup ricotta cheese
   1 egg, beaten

**1.** In a large bowl, dissolve yeast in warm water. Add 2 cups flour, whole wheat flour, brown sugar, oil, egg and salt. Beat on medium speed for 3 minutes. Beat until smooth. Stir in enough remaining flour to form a firm dough.

**2.** Turn onto a floured surface; knead until smooth and elastic, about 6-8 minutes. Place in a greased bowl, turning once to grease the top. Cover and let rise in a warm place until doubled, about 1 hour.

**3.** Meanwhile, in a small skillet, saute mushrooms and garlic in butter until tender; set aside. Punch dough down. Roll into an 18-in. x 12-in. rectangle. Spread ricotta to within 1/2 in. of edges. Sprinkle with mushroom mixture. Roll up jelly-roll style, starting with a short side; pinch seams to seal and tuck ends under. Place seam side down on a greased baking sheet. Cover and let rise until doubled, about 40 minutes.

**4.** Brush with egg. Bake at 350° for 30-35 minutes or until golden brown. Cool for 10 minutes before removing from pan to a wire rack to cool completely. Refrigerate leftovers. **Yield:** 1 loaf (17 slices).

# Cheesecake Pumpkin Muffins

*My mother-in-law came up with these tender treats by combining a few of her favorite recipes. The muffins are chock-full of pumpkin and feature both a sweet cream cheese filling and a crunchy praline topping.* *–Lisa Powelson, Scott City, Kansas*

   3 cups all-purpose flour
   2 cups sugar
   2 teaspoons baking soda
   2 teaspoons baking powder
   1 teaspoon salt
   1 teaspoon ground cinnamon
   4 eggs
   1 can (15 ounces) solid-pack pumpkin
 1-1/2 cups canola oil
CREAM CHEESE FILLING:
   1 package (8 ounces) cream cheese, softened

1/2 cup sugar
    1 egg
    1 tablespoon all-purpose flour
PRALINE TOPPING:
    2/3 cup chopped pecans
    1/3 cup packed brown sugar
    2 tablespoons sour cream

**1.** In a large bowl, combine the first six ingredients. In another bowl, whisk the eggs, pumpkin and oil. Stir into dry ingredients just until moistened. Fill greased or paper-lined muffin cups one-third full.

**2.** For filling, beat the cream cheese, sugar, egg and flour until smooth. Drop by tablespoonfuls into center of each muffin. Top with remaining batter.

**3.** For topping, in a small bowl, combine the pecans, brown sugar and sour cream; spoon over batter. Bake at 400° for 15-18 minutes or until a toothpick comes out clean. Cool for 5 minutes before removing from pans to wire racks. Serve warm. Refrigerate leftovers. **Yield:** 2 dozen.

*Jumbo Jalapeno Cheddar Rolls*

# Cornmeal Yeast Rolls

*These moist rolls have a glossy, golden color and a sweet cornmeal flavor. They're perfect alongside chili, soup or stew on a cold winter's night…and no one will guess that the recipe uses low-fat ingredients.* ~Margaret Wagner Allen, Abingdon, Virginia

    1 package (1/4 ounce) active dry yeast
    1/4 cup warm water (110° to 115°)
1-3/4 cups warm skim milk (110° to 115°)
1-1/2 cups cornmeal
    1/2 cup egg substitute
    1/3 cup sugar
    1/4 cup canola oil
    1/4 cup reduced-fat butter, melted
    1 teaspoon salt
    5 to 5-1/2 cups all-purpose flour
Additional melted reduced-fat butter, optional

**1.** In a large bowl, dissolve yeast in warm water. Add the milk, cornmeal, egg substitute, sugar, oil, butter, salt and 2 cups flour; beat until smooth. Stir in enough remaining flour to form a soft dough (dough will be sticky).

**2.** Turn onto a floured surface; knead until smooth and elastic, about 6-8 minutes. Place in a bowl coated with cooking spray, turning once to coat the top. Cover and let rise in a warm place until doubled, about 1 hour.

**3.** Punch dough down. Divide into six portions. Divide each into 12 pieces. Shape each into a ball; place two balls in each muffin cup coated with cooking spray. Cover and let rise in a warm place until doubled, about 45 minutes.

**4.** Bake at 375° for 10-12 minutes or until golden brown. Lightly brush with additional melted butter if desired. Remove from pans to wire racks to cool. **Yield:** 3 dozen.

**Editor's Note:** This recipe was tested with Land O'Lakes light stick butter.

# Jumbo Jalapeno Cheddar Rolls

*Add color to your Christmas or New Year's spread with these pretty rolls. The cheese and pepper accents are mild but result in a zesty taste.* ~Linda Foreman, Locust Grove, Oklahoma

    2 packages (1/4 ounce *each*) active dry yeast
    2 tablespoons sugar
    2 cups warm milk (110° to 115°)
    2 eggs
    2 teaspoons salt
6-1/2 to 7-1/2 cups all-purpose flour
    2 cups (8 ounces) shredded cheddar cheese
    1/4 cup chopped seeded jalapeno pepper
EGG WASH:
    1 egg
    2 teaspoons water

**1.** In a large bowl, dissolve yeast and sugar in warm milk. Add the eggs, salt and 4 cups flour. Beat on medium speed for 3 minutes. Add cheese and jalapeno. Stir in enough remaining flour to form a firm dough.

**2.** Turn onto a floured surface; knead until smooth and elastic, about 6-8 minutes. Place in a greased bowl, turning once to grease the top. Cover and let rise in a warm place until doubled, about 1 hour.

**3.** Punch dough down. Turn onto a lightly floured surface; divide into 12 pieces. Shape each into a roll. Place 3 in. apart on lightly greased baking sheets. Cover and let rise until doubled, about 30 minutes.

**4.** Combine egg and water; brush over rolls. Bake at 375° for 16-20 minutes or until golden brown. Remove from pans to wire racks. Serve warm. **Yield:** 1 dozen.

**Editor's Note:** When cutting hot peppers, disposable gloves are recommended. Avoid touching your face.

*Whole Wheat Cranberry Scones*

## Whole Wheat Cranberry Scones

*The hearty texture of these sweet-tart treats makes them perfect for spreading with butter or jelly. Serve the festive, cranberry-dotted scones at your next breakfast or brunch...or simply enjoy them as an afternoon snack with a hot cup of tea.*
*~Patsye Yonce, Ovid, New York*

1-1/2 cups all-purpose flour
1-1/2 cups whole wheat flour
 1/2 cup sugar
  3 teaspoons baking powder
 1/2 teaspoon baking soda
 1/2 teaspoon salt
 1/4 teaspoon ground nutmeg
 3/4 cup cold butter
  1 egg
  1 cup vanilla yogurt
 1/2 teaspoon vanilla extract
  1 cup dried cranberries
  1 tablespoon milk
  2 teaspoons cinnamon-sugar

**1.** In a large bowl, combine the flours, sugar, baking powder, baking soda, salt and nutmeg; cut in butter until crumbly. In a small bowl, combine the egg, yogurt and vanilla; stir into dry ingredients just until moistened. Stir in cranberries. Turn onto a floured surface, knead 6-8 times.

**2.** Divide dough in half. Transfer each portion to a greased baking sheet. Pat into an 8-in. circle. Cut each circle into 8 wedges, but do not separate. Brush with milk; sprinkle with cinnamon-sugar. Bake at 400° for 15-20 minutes or until golden brown. Serve warm. **Yield:** 16 scones.

## Cinnamon Crescent Rolls

*I always whip up these flaky, buttery crescents to take to family gatherings at Christmastime. With a luscious cinnamon filling and sweet glaze drizzled on top, these rolls are sure to have you baking batch after batch for your own holiday get-togethers.*
*~Sharon McKee, Denton, Texas*

6-1/2 to 7 cups all-purpose flour
  2 packages (1/4 ounce *each*) active dry yeast
  2 tablespoons sugar
  1 teaspoon salt
  1 cup butter, cubed
  1 can (12 ounces) evaporated milk
 1/2 cup shortening
 1/4 cup water
  3 egg yolks
FILLING:
 1/2 cup sugar
1-1/2 teaspoons ground cinnamon
 1/2 cup butter, softened, *divided*
GLAZE:
  2 cups confectioners' sugar
  3 to 4 tablespoons milk
 1/2 teaspoon vanilla extract
  2 tablespoons sugar
 1/2 teaspoon ground cinnamon

**1.** In a large bowl, combine 3 cups flour, yeast, sugar and salt. In a large saucepan, heat the butter, evaporated milk, shortening and water to 120°-130°. Add to dry ingredients; beat just until moistened. Add egg yolks; beat until smooth. Stir in enough remaining flour to form a soft dough (dough will be sticky).

**2.** Turn onto a floured surface; knead until smooth and elastic, about 6-8 minutes. Place in a greased bowl, turning once to grease top. Cover and let rise in a warm place until doubled, about 1 hour. In a small bowl, combine sugar and cinnamon; set aside.

**3.** Punch dough down. Turn onto a lightly floured surface; knead about six times. Divide dough into four portions. Roll out one portion into a 12-in. circle; spread with 2 tablespoons butter and sprinkle with 2 tablespoons cinnamon-sugar. Cut into 12 wedges. Roll up each from the wide end and place point side down 3 in. apart on ungreased baking sheets. Curve ends to form crescents.

**4.** Repeat with the remaining dough, butter and cinnamon-sugar. Cover and let rise until doubled, about 45 minutes. Bake at 350° for 15-20 minutes or until lightly browned. Remove to wire racks. Combine the confectioners' sugar, milk and vanilla; drizzle over warm rolls. Combine sugar and cinnamon; sprinkle over rolls. **Yield:** 4 dozen.

Cinnamon Crescent Rolls

# Cinnamon-Glazed Braid

*After tasting an unforgettably delicious bread in a Portland deli, I set out to duplicate the recipe so I could make it at home. I came up with this tender braid that my wife and I often make for potlucks or to give as a gift.* ~Ken Lang, Dayville, Oregon

    1 egg
  1/4 cup butter, softened
3-1/2 cups bread flour
  1/3 cup sugar
    1 teaspoon salt
    1 package (1/4 ounce) active dry yeast
CINNAMON GLAZE:
    1 cup confectioners' sugar
  1/2 teaspoon ground cinnamon
  1/2 teaspoon vanilla extract
    2 to 3 tablespoons milk

**1.** Place egg in a measuring cup; add enough water (70°-80°) to measure 1 cup. In bread machine pan, place egg mixture, butter, bread flour, sugar, salt and yeast in the order suggested by the manufacturer. Select dough setting (check dough after 5 minutes of mixing; add 1 to 2 tablespoons of water or flour if needed).

**2.** When cycle is completed, turn dough onto a lightly floured surface. Divide into thirds. Roll each portion into a 13-in. rope. Place ropes on a greased baking sheet and braid; pinch seams firmly to seal and tuck ends under. Cover and let rise in a warm place until doubled, about 45 minutes.

**3.** Bake at 350° for 20-25 minutes or until golden brown. Remove from pan to a wire rack. Cool for 10 minutes. Combine the glaze ingredients; drizzle over bread. **Yield:** 1 loaf (1-1/2 pounds).

*Cinnamon-Glazed Braid*

# Upside-Down Peach Bread

*This impressive, fruit-filled loaf may remind you of an upside-down cake and is sure to attract attention on your holiday buffet table. The cream cheese makes it rich—and even more impossible to resist!* ~Becky Tackett, Porter, Oklahoma

    1 package (16 ounces) frozen unsweetened sliced
       peaches, thawed
  1/4 cup butter, melted
  1/4 cup packed brown sugar
1-1/2 cups chopped pecans, *divided*
1-1/2 teaspoons ground cinnamon, *divided*
  3/4 cup butter, softened
    4 ounces cream cheese, softened
    2 cups sugar
    2 eggs
    1 teaspoon almond extract
    1 teaspoon vanilla extract
    3 cups all-purpose flour
    1 teaspoon baking powder
  1/2 teaspoon baking soda
  1/2 teaspoon salt

**1.** Thinly slice half of the peaches; chop remaining peaches. Set aside.

**2.** Pour melted butter into two greased 9-in. x 5-in. loaf pans; sprinkle with brown sugar. Arrange peach slices cut side down in a single layer over brown sugar. Sprinkle with 1/2 cup pecans and 1/2 teaspoon cinnamon; set aside.

**3.** In a large bowl, cream the butter, cream cheese and sugar until light and fluffy. Add eggs and extracts; mix well.

**4.** Combine the flour, baking powder, baking soda, salt and remaining cinnamon; add to creamed mixture. Fold in chopped peaches and remaining pecans.

**5.** Transfer batter to prepared pans. Bake at 350° for 45-55 minutes or until a toothpick inserted near the center comes out clean. Cool for 10 minutes before inverting onto serving plates. Serve warm. **Yield:** 2 loaves (12 slices each).

# Pecan Apple Loaves

*Loaded with chopped tart apples and pecans, this is a quick bread recipe you'll want to permanently add to your Christmas recipe file. The blend of cinnamon, cloves and nutmeg enhances the yummy flavor.* ~Lois Smith, Irvington, Illinois

    3 cups all-purpose flour
    2 cups sugar
    2 teaspoons baking soda
  3/4 teaspoon ground cinnamon
  1/4 teaspoon salt
  1/4 teaspoon ground nutmeg
  1/4 teaspoon ground cloves
    2 eggs
    1 cup butter, melted
    2 teaspoons vanilla extract
    4 cups chopped peeled tart apples
    1 cup chopped pecans

1. In a large bowl, combine the flour, sugar, baking soda, cinnamon, salt, nutmeg and cloves. In another bowl, whisk the eggs, butter and vanilla until blended. Stir into dry ingredients just until moistened. (Mixture will be stiff.) Fold in apples and pecans.

2. Pour into two greased and floured 9-in. x 5-in. loaf pans. Bake at 325° for 70-80 minutes or until a toothpick inserted near the center comes out clean. Cool for 10 minutes before removing from pans to wire racks. **Yield:** 2 loaves (16 slices each).

# Cherry Chocolate Chip Bread

*This heavenly loaf dotted with dark chocolate chips, maraschino cherries and hazelnuts will sweeten any holiday meal. Serve it in place of the usual fruitcake for a decadent delight.*
*–David Dahlman, Chatsworth, California*

*Onion Dill Bread*

2-1/2 cups all-purpose flour
  1/2 cup sugar
  1/2 cup packed brown sugar
    1 teaspoon baking powder
    1 teaspoon baking soda
    1 teaspoon salt
    1 egg
1-1/4 cups evaporated milk
    3 tablespoons canola oil
    1 teaspoon vanilla extract
  1/2 cup dark chocolate chips
  1/2 cup hazelnuts, coarsely chopped
  1/2 cup coarsely chopped maraschino cherries

1. In a large bowl, combine the flour, sugars, baking powder, baking soda and salt. In a small bowl, whisk the egg, evaporated milk, oil and vanilla. Stir into the dry ingredients just until moistened. Fold in the chocolate chips, hazelnuts and maraschino cherries.

2. Transfer to a greased 9-in. x 5-in. loaf pan. Bake at 350° for 55-60 minutes or until a toothpick inserted near the center comes out clean. Cool for 10 minutes before removing from pan to a wire rack. **Yield:** 1 loaf (16 slices).

# Onion Dill Bread

*You'll hear "Mmmm!" all around when guests bite into this savory loaf. Made in a bread machine, it's crisp and golden brown on the outside but moist and tender on the inside. The dill and onion make it flavorful without overwhelming your taste buds.*
*~Charlotte Elliot, Neenah, Wisconsin*

1-1/2 cups water (70° to 80°)
    2 tablespoons olive oil, *divided*
  1/4 cup dried minced onion
    2 teaspoons sugar
1-1/4 teaspoons salt
    1 teaspoon dill weed
  1/2 teaspoon onion powder
3-1/2 cups all-purpose flour
  3/4 cup whole wheat flour
    1 package (1/4 ounce) active dry yeast

1. In bread machine pan, place the water, 1 tablespoon oil, minced onion, sugar, salt, dill, onion powder, flours and yeast in the order suggested by manufacturer. Select dough setting (check dough after 5 minutes of mixing; add 1 to 2 tablespoons of water or flour if needed).

2. When cycle is completed, turn dough onto a lightly floured surface. Divide dough in half; shape each portion into a 7-in. round loaf. Place on greased baking sheets. Cover and let rise until doubled, about 40 minutes.

3. Bake at 400° for 15-20 minutes or until golden brown. Brush with remaining oil. Remove from pans to wire racks. **Yield:** 2 loaves (9 slices each).

# Bacon Onion Bread

*This simple, great-tasting bread is a terrific one to put out for company at a special dinner...or to slice for sandwiches at a casual party. Just put the ingredients in the bread machine and let it do all the work.* *~Anna Free, Fairbanks, Alaska*

1-1/4 cups water (70° to 80°)
    2 teaspoons butter
    5 tablespoons dried minced onion
    2 tablespoons sugar
    1 teaspoon salt
  1/4 teaspoon ground allspice
  1/4 cup finely crumbled cooked bacon
4-1/2 teaspoons nonfat dry milk powder
    3 cups all-purpose flour
    2 teaspoons active dry yeast

In bread machine pan, place all ingredients in order suggested by manufacturer. Select French bread setting. Choose crust color and loaf size if available. Bake according to bread machine directions (check dough after 5 minutes of mixing; add 1 to 2 tablespoons water or flour if needed). **Yield:** 1 loaf (1-1/2 pounds).

**Editor's Note:** We recommend you do not use a bread machine's time-delay feature for this recipe.

*Stuffed Cherry Tomatoes Two Ways (p. 45)*
*Rumaki Appetizers*
*Swiss Seafood Canapes*

# Elegant Appetizers

*Entertaining during the Christmas season calls for hors d'oeuvres that are extra special. Look here for memorable munchies guests are sure to love.*

## Swiss Seafood Canapes

*If you're the cook, you'll want to set a few of these aside for yourself before serving them at a party. They disappear fast! The broiled bites feature a cheesy mixture of crab and shrimp.*
~Del Mason, Martensville, Saskatchewan

1 can (6 ounces) small shrimp, rinsed and drained
1 package (6 ounces) frozen crabmeat, thawed
1 cup (4 ounces) shredded Swiss cheese
2 hard-cooked eggs, chopped
1/4 cup finely chopped celery
1/4 cup mayonnaise
1/4 cup French salad dressing *or* seafood cocktail sauce
2 green onions, chopped
Dash salt
1 loaf (16 ounces) snack rye bread

In a large bowl, combine first nine ingredients. Place bread on ungreased baking sheets. Broil 4-6 in. from the heat for 1-2 minutes or until lightly browned. Turn slices; spread each with 1 rounded tablespoonful of seafood mixture. Broil 4-5 minutes longer or until heated through. **Yield:** 4 dozen.

## Rumaki Appetizers

*These are a Christmas-season "must" in our family. Wrapped in bacon, the appetizers are served with a simple, sweet barbecue sauce...which also goes well with little smoked sausages.*
~Janice Thomas, Milford, Nebraska

1 cup packed brown sugar
1/2 cup mayonnaise
1/2 cup chili sauce
13 bacon strips, cut into thirds
1 can (8 ounces) whole water chestnuts, drained
1 can (8 ounces) pineapple chunks, drained

In a small saucepan, combine the brown sugar, mayonnaise and chili sauce. Cook and stir until mixture comes to a boil; set aside. Wrap a bacon piece around water chestnut and pineapple; secure with a toothpick. Broil until bacon is crisp, about 5 minutes; turn. Broil 4 minutes longer or until bacon is crisp. Serve with sauce. **Yield:** 39 appetizers.

## Chicken Salad in Baskets

*When I first came across the recipe for these cute little cups years ago, I couldn't believe that pineapple, onion and green pepper would make a tasty combination. Was I surprised!*
~Gwendolyn Fae Trapp, Strongsville, Ohio

1 cup diced cooked chicken
3 bacon strips, cooked and crumbled
1/3 cup chopped mushrooms
2 tablespoons chopped pecans
2 tablespoons diced peeled apple
1/4 cup mayonnaise
1/8 teaspoon salt
Dash pepper
20 slices bread
6 tablespoons butter, melted
2 tablespoons minced fresh parsley

**1.** In a small bowl, combine the first five ingredients. Combine the mayonnaise, salt and pepper; add to chicken mixture and stir to coat. Cover and refrigerate until serving.

**2.** Cut each slice of bread with a 3-in. round cookie cutter; brush both sides with butter. Press into ungreased mini muffin cups. Bake at 350° for 11-13 minutes or until golden brown and crisp.

**3.** Cool for 3 minutes before removing from pans to wire racks to cool completely. Spoon 1 tablespoonful chicken salad into each bread basket. Cover and refrigerate for up to 2 hours. Just before serving, sprinkle with parsley. **Yield:** 20 appetizers.

*Chicken Salad in Baskets*

## Sweet & Sour Chicken Wings

*Enjoy these lip-smacking wings at Christmas parties, but keep the recipe in mind for your summertime get-togethers, too. It's great year-round!* ~Connie Vander Ploeg, Sioux Center, Iowa

2 cups sugar
2 cups water
2 cups soy sauce
1 cup unsweetened pineapple juice
1/2 cup canola oil
2 teaspoons garlic powder
2 teaspoons ground ginger
8 pounds frozen chicken wingettes and drumettes, thawed

**1.** In a large resealable plastic bag, combine the first seven ingredients. Add the chicken wings; seal bag and toss to coat. Refrigerate for 8 hours or overnight.

**2.** Drain and discard the marinade. Place the chicken wings in two greased 15-in. x 10-in. baking pans. Cover and bake at 350° for 40-45 minutes or until the juices run clear. **Yield:** about 5-1/2 dozen.

## Raspberry Chipotle Dip

*Guests are amazed when I tell them this scrumptious, attractive cheese dip uses only three ingredients. Just add your favorite crackers, and you'll have a hit.* ~Pat Stevens, Granbury, Texas

3 cartons (8 ounces *each*) whipped cream cheese
1 cup raspberry chipotle salsa
1/2 cup pecan halves, toasted
Assorted crackers

Spread cream cheese onto a small serving platter. Top with salsa and pecans. Refrigerate until serving. Serve with crackers. **Yield:** 3 cups.

**Editor's Note:** This recipe was tested with Mrs. Renfro's raspberry chipotle salsa.

## Sharp Cheddar Turnovers

*These savory little snacks are so good, it's difficult to eat just one! With cheese peeking out from the golden brown pastry, they're irresistible.* ~Lynn Roberts, Cantonment, Florida

1 package (8 ounces) cream cheese, softened
1 tablespoon butter
2 teaspoons water
1-1/4 cups all-purpose flour
2 cups (8 ounces) shredded sharp cheddar cheese
2 eggs

**1.** In a large bowl, beat the cream cheese, butter and water until smooth. Gradually beat in flour until blended. Shape into a ball, then flatten into a disk. Wrap in plastic wrap; refrigerate for 30 minutes.

**2.** In a small bowl, combine cheese and 1 egg. On a lightly floured surface, roll out dough to 1/8-in. thickness. Cut with a floured 3-in. round cookie cutter. Place 1 teaspoon of filling on one side of each circle. Moisten edges; fold dough over filling and press edges together firmly with a fork to seal.

**3.** Place on greased baking sheets. Beat remaining egg; brush over turnovers. Bake at 400° for 20-25 minutes or until golden brown. Serve warm. Refrigerate leftovers. **Yield:** 2-1/2 dozen.

## Pumpkin Bread With Fruit Topping

*This unusual appetizer is popular with all ages. The pumpkin toasts are almost like little cookies, topped with wonderfully spiced fruit. You could even serve these as a dessert with hot cider or cocoa.* ~Adam Carlson, Liberty Boro, Pennsylvania

6 tablespoons butter, softened
1-1/3 cups sugar
2 eggs
1 cup canned pumpkin
1/2 teaspoon vanilla extract
1-1/2 cups all-purpose flour
1-1/2 teaspoons baking powder
1-1/2 teaspoons ground cinnamon
1 teaspoon salt
1 teaspoon ground ginger
1/2 teaspoon ground nutmeg
1/4 teaspoon baking soda
1/4 teaspoon ground cloves
TOPPING:
1 cup apple pie filling, chopped
1/2 cup raisins
1/2 cup dried cranberries

Raspberry Chipotle Dip

2 tablespoons molasses
1/2 teaspoon *each* ground ginger, cinnamon, nutmeg
  and cloves
1 teaspoon cornstarch
1/2 cup apple cider *or* juice

**1.** In a large bowl, beat butter and sugar until crumbly, about 2 minutes. Beat in eggs, pumpkin and vanilla. Combine flour, baking powder, cinnamon, salt, ginger, nutmeg, baking soda and cloves; add to butter mixture just until blended.

**2.** Transfer to three greased 5-3/4-in. x 3-in. loaf pans. Bake at 350° for 30-35 minutes or until a toothpick inserted near the center comes out clean. Cool for 10 minutes before removing from pans to wire racks to cool completely.

**3.** Transfer loaves to a cutting board; cut into 1/2-in. slices. Place cut side down on ungreased baking sheets. Bake for 5-10 minutes on each side or until lightly browned and firm. Remove to wire racks to cool.

**4.** In a small saucepan, combine pie filling, raisins, cranberries, molasses and spices. Bring to a boil over medium heat, stirring constantly. Combine the cornstarch and cider until smooth; stir into apple mixture. Return to a boil; cook for 1-2 minutes or until thickened. Remove from the heat; cool. Serve with toast. **Yield:** 2-1/2 dozen.

# Cranberry Spread

*The orange-cranberry combination is the key to this refreshing cream-cheese spread. Chopped pecans add even more Christmastime flair.* ~Sharman Pittman, Asheville, North Carolina

1 package (8 ounces) cream cheese, softened
2 tablespoons orange juice concentrate
1 tablespoon sugar
4 teaspoons grated orange peel
1/8 teaspoon ground cinnamon
1/4 cup finely chopped dried cranberries
1/4 cup finely chopped pecans
Assorted crackers

In a small bowl, beat the cream cheese, orange juice concentrate, sugar, peel and cinnamon until blended. Fold in cranberries and pecans. Cover and refrigerate for at least 1 hour. Serve with crackers. **Yield:** 1-1/2 cups.

# Carrot Fritters

*Crispy and mild-flavored, this fun finger food always gets snatched up quickly. If there are any leftovers, they reheat well for a snack the next day.* ~Susan Witt, Fairbury, Nebraska

1 cup all-purpose flour
1 teaspoon salt
1 teaspoon baking powder
2 eggs
1/2 cup milk
1 teaspoon canola oil
3 cups shredded carrots
Oil for deep-fat frying

*Carrot Fritters*

**1.** In a large bowl, combine the flour, salt and baking powder. Combine the eggs, milk and oil; add to dry ingredients just until moistened. Fold in carrots.

**2.** In an electric skillet, heat 1/4 in. of oil to 375°. Drop batter by 2 tablespoonfuls into hot oil; press lightly to flatten. Fry until golden brown, about 1-2 minutes on each side. Drain on paper towels. **Yield:** 20 fritters.

# Stuffed Cherry Tomatoes Two Ways

*With both a shrimp and bacon version, this recipe gives you two delicious appetizers in one. The bright red tomatoes look so festive on a holiday buffet.* ~Arlene Kay Butler, Ogden, Utah

2 pints cherry tomatoes
CREAM CHEESE & SHRIMP:
4 ounces cream cheese, softened
2 tablespoons ketchup
1/2 teaspoon dill weed
1/3 pound cooked small shrimp, peeled and deveined
Fresh dill sprigs
GUACAMOLE & BACON:
1 medium ripe avocado, peeled
1 tablespoon finely chopped onion
4 teaspoons lemon juice
1 garlic clove, minced
3 bacon strips, cooked and crumbled

**1.** Cut a thin slice off the bottom of each tomato with a sharp knife to allow it to sit flat. Cut a thin slice off the top of each tomato. Scoop out and discard pulp; invert tomatoes onto paper towels to drain.

**2. For shrimp tomatoes:** In a small bowl, combine cream cheese, ketchup and dill weed. Spoon into half of tomatoes. Top with shrimp and dill sprigs. Refrigerate until serving.

**3. For bacon tomatoes:** In a small bowl, mash avocado; stir in onion, juice and garlic. Spoon into half of tomatoes. Top with bacon. Refrigerate until serving. **Yield:** about 4 dozen.

*Roasted Goose with Savory Garlic Stuffing*

# Dazzling Dinners

## Roasted Goose with Savory Garlic Stuffing

*Want an unforgettable entree for Christmas dinner? This tender stuffed bird is the one! The meat stays moist, and the bacon flavor really shines through.* ~Jolie Stinson, Lebanon, Oregon

    1 medium lemon
    1 domestic goose (11 to 13 pounds)
    1/4 teaspoon salt
    1/4 teaspoon pepper
    3 bacon strips
STUFFING:
    2 small onions, finely chopped
    2 celery ribs, chopped
    8 garlic cloves, minced
    1/4 cup butter, cubed
    1 package (14 ounces) seasoned stuffing cubes
    4-1/2 teaspoons dried sage leaves
    3/4 teaspoon salt
    1/2 teaspoon pepper
    1/2 teaspoon *each* dried oregano, thyme and Italian
        seasoning
    1-1/4 cups chicken broth, *divided*
    1/2 cup egg substitute

**1.** Cut lemon in half. Rub inside and outside of goose with cut sides of lemon; discard lemon. Sprinkle inside and outside with salt and pepper. Prick skin well. With fingers, carefully loosen skin from breast; place bacon under skin. Set aside.

**2.** For stuffing, in a large skillet, saute the onions, celery and garlic in butter until tender. Transfer to a large bowl; stir in the stuffing cubes, sage, salt, pepper and herbs. Add 1 cup broth and egg substitute; toss gently. Stuff the goose body and neck cavities loosely; tie drumsticks together.

**3.** Place remaining stuffing in a greased 2-qt. baking dish; drizzle with remaining broth. Cover and refrigerate. Remove from the refrigerator 30 minutes before baking.

**4.** Place goose breast side up on a rack in a roasting pan. Bake, uncovered, at 425° for 30 minutes. Reduce heat to 350°. Bake, uncovered, 2-3/4 to 3 hours longer or until juices run clear and a meat thermometer reads 180° for goose and 165° for stuffing, pricking skin occasionally. (Cover loosely with foil if goose browns too quickly.) If necessary, drain fat from pan as it accumulates.

**5.** Bake additional stuffing, covered, for 25-30 minutes. Uncover; bake 10 minutes longer or until lightly browned. Cover goose with foil and let stand for 20 minutes before removing stuffing and carving goose. **Yield:** 12 servings (12 cups stuffing).

## Roasted Fall Vegetables

*I love serving this slightly spicy dish as part of a comforting dinner on a chilly night. The cayenne pepper lends a nice kick that's not overpowering.* ~Juli Meyers, Sioux City, Iowa

    1 large acorn squash, peeled and cut into 1-1/2-inch
        cubes
    1 large rutabaga, peeled and cut into 1-inch cubes
    1 medium pie pumpkin *or* butternut squash, peeled
        and cut into 1-inch cubes
    3 large carrots, peeled and cut into 1-1/2-inch pieces
    1 medium parsnip, peeled and cut into 1-inch cubes
    1/4 cup grated Parmesan cheese
    1/4 cup canola oil
    3 tablespoons minced fresh parsley
    2 tablespoons paprika
    2 teaspoons salt
    1 teaspoon garlic powder
    1/2 teaspoon cayenne pepper

**1.** In a large bowl, combine the first five ingredients. In a small bowl, combine the remaining ingredients. Pour over vegetables; toss to coat.

**2.** Transfer to two greased 15-in. x 10-in. baking pans. Bake, uncovered, at 425° for 40-50 minutes or until tender, stirring occasionally. **Yield:** 14 servings.

*Roasted Fall Vegetables*

# Orange Cheesecake Dessert

*Indulge your taste buds with these heavenly cheesecake squares featuring the tongue-tingling combination of orange and a hint of almond. The sweet raspberry topping is the crowning touch.*
~Patricia Harmon, Baden, Pennsylvania

1-3/4 cups shortbread cookie crumbs (about 22 cookies)
2/3 cup sliced almonds, finely chopped
2 tablespoons plus 1 cup sugar, *divided*
1/3 cup butter, melted
4 packages (8 ounces *each*) cream cheese, softened
1/2 cup orange juice concentrate
1-1/4 teaspoons almond extract
4 eggs, lightly beaten
2 packages (10 ounces *each*) frozen sweetened raspberries, thawed
2 tablespoons cornstarch

**1.** In a small bowl, combine the shortbread cookie crumbs, almonds and 2 tablespoons sugar; stir in butter. Press into a greased 13-in. x 9-in. baking dish. Cover and refrigerate for at least 15 minutes.

**2.** In a large bowl, beat cream cheese and remaining sugar until smooth. Add orange juice concentrate and extract; beat until smooth. Add eggs; beat on low speed just until combined. Pour over crust.

**3.** Bake at 350° for 35-40 minutes or until center is almost set. Cool on a wire rack for 1 hour. Cover and refrigerate for 8 hours or overnight.

**4.** Drain raspberries, reserving juice; set berries aside. In a small saucepan, combine cornstarch and reserved juice until smooth. Bring to a boil; cook and stir for 1-2 minutes or until thickened. Remove from the heat; gently stir in raspberries. Cool. Serve over cheesecake dessert. **Yield:** 18 servings.

*Orange Cheesecake Dessert*

# Glazed Ham With Cherry Sauce

(Pictured on page 51)

*Every time I serve this mouth-watering smoked ham with a festive cherry sauce, it's a big hit. The glaze adds an impressive, glossy shine.* ~Gloria Warczak, Cedarburg, Wisconsin

1 fully cooked bone-in ham (about 10 pounds)
GLAZE:
1/2 cup packed brown sugar
1 tablespoon cornstarch
1/2 teaspoon ground mustard
1 cup cherry *or* cranberry juice
SAUCE:
6 tablespoons brown sugar
1/4 cup cornstarch
1/2 teaspoon ground cinnamon
1/4 teaspoon ground cloves
2 cups unsweetened apple juice
2 tablespoons cider vinegar
2 cans (14-1/2 ounces *each*) pitted tart cherries, drained
12 to 16 drops red food coloring, optional

**1.** Place ham on a rack in large roasting pan. Bake, uncovered, at 325° for 2 hours.

**2.** For the glaze, in a small saucepan, combine the brown sugar, cornstarch and ground mustard. Stir in the cherry juice until smooth. Bring to a boil over medium heat. Cook and stir for 2 minutes or until thickened. Spoon glaze over the ham. Bake 30-45 minutes longer or until a meat thermometer reaches 140° and ham is heated through. Remove from the oven; keep warm.

**3.** For cherry sauce, in a large saucepan, combine the brown sugar, cornstarch, cinnamon and cloves. Stir in apple juice and vinegar until smooth. Bring to a boil. Cook and stir for 2 minutes or until thickened. Reduce heat. Stir in cherries and food coloring if desired; heat through. Serve with ham. **Yield:** 18 servings (4 cups sauce).

# Coffee Ice Cream Pie

*This luscious ice cream pie boasts a meringue crust and is topped with a smooth caramel sauce. Because it can be made ahead of time and stored in the freezer, it's the perfect dessert to rely on during the hustle and bustle of the holiday season.*
~Diane Morin, Hearst, Ontario

2 egg whites
1/2 teaspoon vanilla extract
1/4 teaspoon cream of tartar
1/4 teaspoon salt
1/2 cup sugar
1/2 cup finely chopped pecans
1 pint vanilla ice cream, softened
1 pint coffee ice cream, softened
CARAMEL SAUCE:
1 cup packed brown sugar

1 can (5 ounces) evaporated milk
3 tablespoons butter
Dash salt
1/2 cup golden raisins
1 teaspoon vanilla extract

**1.** For meringue, place egg whites in a small bowl; let stand at room temperature for 30 minutes. Add the vanilla, cream of tartar and salt; beat until soft peaks form. Gradually beat in sugar, 1 tablespoon at a time, on high until stiff peaks form. Fold in pecans.

**2.** Spread meringue onto the bottom and up the sides of a greased 9-in. pie plate. Bake at 250° for 1 hour or until light golden brown. Turn oven off; leave meringue shell in oven for 1 hour. Cool on a wire rack. Spoon ice cream into meringue shell. Cover and freeze at least 4 hours or until firm.

**3.** Remove from the freezer 15 minutes before serving. In a small saucepan, combine the brown sugar, milk, butter and salt. Cook and stir over medium-low heat for 4-5 minutes or until sauce comes to a boil. Remove from the heat; stir in raisins and vanilla. Serve warm sauce with pie. **Yield:** 8 servings (1-1/2 cups sauce).

*Italian Baked Chicken*

## Pepper and Mushroom Corn Pudding

*Here's a comforting, home-style dish that turns ordinary meals into something to celebrate. It can be presented as a side, but it's also hearty enough to enjoy as a meatless main course.*
*~Carole Resnick, Cleveland, Ohio*

1 pound sliced baby portobello mushrooms
3 tablespoons finely chopped green pepper
3 tablespoons finely chopped sweet red pepper
2 tablespoons olive oil
5 cups frozen corn, thawed, *divided*
5 ounces cream cheese, cubed
1/2 cup yellow cornmeal
2 tablespoons sugar
6 eggs, beaten
3/4 pound Gruyere cheese, shredded, *divided*
1 can (14-3/4 ounces) cream-style corn
1 cup heavy whipping cream
3/4 teaspoon salt

**1.** In a large skillet, saute mushrooms and peppers in oil until tender. Remove and set aside.

**2.** In a food processor, combine 2 cups whole kernel corn, cream cheese, cornmeal and sugar; cover and process until smooth. In large bowl, combine the eggs, 1-1/2 cups shredded Gruyere cheese, cream-style corn, cream and salt. Stir in processed corn mixture, reserved mushroom mixture and remaining corn until well blended.

**3.** Transfer to a greased 13-in. x 9-in. baking dish; sprinkle with remaining cheese. Bake, uncovered, at 375° for 45-55 minutes or until a knife inserted near the center comes out clean. **Yield:** 13 servings.

## Italian Baked Chicken

*This zesty chicken is a favorite for casual Christmastime meals. Served over angel hair pasta, it's delicious and a great choice for company.*      *~Marcello Basco, Deerfield Beach, Florida*

1/2 cup all-purpose flour
1/2 teaspoon salt
1/8 teaspoon pepper
4 boneless skinless chicken breast halves (6 ounces *each*)
3 tablespoons olive oil, *divided*
5 garlic cloves, minced
1 teaspoon dried oregano
1 teaspoon dried basil
2 cups chicken broth
1 cup tomato puree
4 slices part-skim mozzarella cheese
4 tomato slices
4 teaspoons grated Parmesan cheese
Hot cooked angel hair pasta
Minced fresh parsley

**1.** In a large resealable plastic bag, combine the flour, salt and pepper; add the chicken, one piece at a time, and shake to coat. In a large skillet over medium heat, brown chicken in 2 tablespoons oil on each side. Transfer to a greased 11-in. x 7-in. baking dish.

**2.** In the same skillet, saute the garlic, oregano and basil in remaining oil for 1 minute. Add broth and tomato puree. Bring to a boil. Remove from heat; pour over chicken. Cover and bake at 400° for 25-30 minutes or until juices run clear.

**3.** Remove chicken and set aside. Pour sauce into a bowl and keep warm. Return chicken to the pan; top each with a cheese and tomato slice. Sprinkle with Parmesan cheese. Bake, uncovered, for 6-8 minutes or until cheese is melted. Arrange pasta on a large serving platter; top with chicken. Pour sauce over chicken and sprinkle with parsley. **Yield:** 4 servings.

*Special Romaine Salad*

# Special Romaine Salad

*This fuss-free romaine salad with homemade croutons is loaded with flavor. Curry powder gives the dressing zip, while three kinds of cheese add richness. Serve plates of these fresh greens to start off Christmas dinner in a mouth-watering way.*
*~Mary Ellen Friend, Ravenswood, West Virginia*

    4 teaspoons olive oil
1/4 teaspoon garlic powder
    3 slices Italian bread (3/4 inch thick), cubed
2/3 cup mayonnaise
    2 tablespoons plus 2 teaspoons buttermilk
    4 teaspoons grated Parmesan cheese
1-1/2 teaspoons onion soup mix
1/8 teaspoon curry powder
1/8 teaspoon anchovy paste
    8 cups torn romaine
1/4 cup crumbled blue cheese
1/2 cup shredded Parmesan cheese

**1.** In a large bowl, combine oil and garlic powder. Add bread cubes; toss to coat. Arrange in a single layer on an ungreased baking sheet. Bake at 325° for 15-20 minutes or until lightly browned, stirring occasionally.

**2.** For salad dressing, in a large bowl, combine the mayonnaise, buttermilk, grated Parmesan cheese, soup mix, curry and anchovy paste. Cover and refrigerate for at least 2 hours.

**3.** In a salad bowl, combine romaine and blue cheese. Drizzle with dressing; toss to coat. Garnish with shredded Parmesan cheese. **Yield:** 10 servings.

# Cloverleaf Wheat Rolls

*With a slightly sweet taste, these attractive goodies will complement just about any holiday menu. The whole wheat dough is easy to prepare, and the rolls come out of the oven light, tender and golden brown.*    *~April Jackson, Edgewood, New Mexico*

    2 packages (1/4 ounce *each*) active dry yeast
    2 cups warm water (110° to 115°)
1/2 cup sugar
1/4 cup shortening
    1 egg
1-1/2 teaspoons salt
    3 cups whole wheat flour
    3 to 3-1/2 cups all-purpose flour

**1.** In a large bowl, dissolve the two packages of yeast in the warm water. Add the sugar, shortening, egg, salt and whole wheat flour. Beat mixture on medium speed until smooth. Stir in enough all-purpose flour to form a soft dough (the dough will be sticky).

**2.** Turn onto a floured surface; knead for 15-20 minutes or until smooth and elastic. Place in a greased bowl, turning once to grease the top. Cover and let rise in a warm place until doubled, about 1 hour.

**3.** Punch the dough down; divide into six portions. Divide each portion into 12 pieces. Shape each piece into a ball; place three balls in each greased muffin cup. Cover and let rise until doubled, about 30 minutes.

**4.** Bake at 350° for 15-20 minutes or until golden brown. Remove from pans to wire racks. **Yield:** 2 dozen.

# Sesame Vegetables

*When I go out to my vegetable garden in summer to "pick" dinner, my family knows I plan to prepare this well-coated, stovetop side dish. It's just as good during cold-weather months using the fresh produce available in the supermarket.*
*~Juanita Golden, Ibecia, Missouri*

    3 cups fresh cauliflowerets
2-1/2 cups cut fresh green beans
    4 cups fresh broccoli florets
3-1/2 cups fresh snow peas
    2 small yellow summer squash, cubed
    2 small zucchini, cubed
    1 small onion, chopped
    3 tablespoons olive oil, *divided*
    1 tablespoon sugar
    1 tablespoon sesame seeds, toasted
    1 tablespoon lemon juice
    1 tablespoon soy sauce

**1.** Place the cauliflower and green beans in a steamer basket; place basket in a large saucepan over 1 in. of water. Bring to a boil; cover and steam for 8-10 minutes or until crisp-tender, adding the broccoli and snow peas during the last 4 minutes.

**2.** Meanwhile, in a small skillet, saute the yellow squash, zucchini and onion in 2 tablespoons oil until tender. Remove from the heat; stir in the sugar, sesame seeds, lemon juice, soy sauce and remaining oil.

**3.** Transfer cauliflower mixture to a large serving bowl; add squash mixture and toss to coat. Serve immediately. **Yield:** 13 servings.

*Cloverleaf Wheat Rolls*
*Sesame Vegetables*
*Glazed Ham with Cherry Sauce (p. 48)*

# Lemon Ricotta Cake

*The recipe for this moist, four-layer cake is a gem that was passed down from my grandmother. Garnished with lemon peel, it's sure to impress.*     *~Nan Slaughter, Sammamish, Washington*

>     3 eggs
>     2 egg yolks
>     2/3 cup sugar
>     1/3 cup lemon juice
>     1/3 cup butter, cubed
> CAKE BATTER:
>     1 cup butter, softened
>     2 cups sugar
>     3 eggs
>     1 cup ricotta cheese
>     1 cup buttermilk
>     1 tablespoon grated lemon peel
> 1-1/2 teaspoons vanilla extract
>     1 teaspoon lemon juice
>     3 cups all-purpose flour
>     1/2 teaspoon baking powder
>     1/2 teaspoon baking soda
>     1/2 teaspoon salt
> SUGARED LEMON PEEL:
>     6 medium lemons
>     1/4 cup sugar
> FROSTING:
>     2/3 cup butter, softened
>     5-1/2 cups confectioners' sugar
>     1/3 cup milk
> 1-1/2 teaspoons grated lemon peel
> 1-1/2 teaspoons vanilla extract
>     1/8 teaspoon salt

**1.** For the lemon curd, in a small bowl, combine the eggs and egg yolks. In a heavy saucepan, cook and stir the sugar, lemon juice and butter over medium heat until smooth. Stir a small amount of the hot mixture into the eggs; return all to the saucepan, stirring constantly. Bring to a gentle boil, cook and stir for 2 minutes. Cool slightly. Cover and chill for 1-1/2 hours or until thickened.

**2.** In a large bowl, cream butter and sugar until light and fluffy. Add eggs, one at a time, beating well after each addition. Combine the ricotta cheese, buttermilk, lemon peel, vanilla and lemon juice. Combine the flour, baking powder, baking soda and salt; add to the creamed mixture alternately with the buttermilk mixture, beating well after each addition.

**3.** Pour into two greased and floured 9-in. round baking pans. Bake at 350° for 30-35 minutes or until a toothpick inserted near the center comes out clean. Cool for 10 minutes before removing from pans to wire racks to cool completely.

**4.** Using a citrus zester, remove the peel from the lemons in long narrow strips; toss the peel with the sugar. Let stand for 30 minutes. (Save the fruit for another use.) Meanwhile, in a large bowl, cream the butter until light and fluffy. Add the confectioners' sugar, milk, lemon peel, vanilla and salt; beat until smooth.

**5.** Cut each cake in half horizontally. Place one cake layer on a serving plate. Pipe a bead of frosting around the edge of the cake. Spread a third of the lemon curd inside the bead of frosting. Repeat layers twice. Top with remaining cake layer. Frost top and sides of cake. Garnish with sugared lemon peel. Store in the refrigerator. **Yield:** 12-16 servings.

*Lemon Ricotta Cake*

# Waldorf Salad Mold

*When I was a girl, my mom would make Waldorf salad for winter holidays using Red Delicious apples. This convenient mold features a citrus dressing and can be prepared ahead of time.*
*~Susan Brown, Northglenn, Colorado*

>     2 packages (3 ounces *each*) strawberry gelatin
>     2 cups boiling water
> 1-1/2 cups cold water
>     2 medium apples, diced
>     1/2 cup chopped celery
>     1/4 cup chopped walnuts
> LEMON YOGURT DRESSING:
>     1 carton (6 ounces) lemon yogurt
> 1-1/2 teaspoons brown sugar
>     1/8 teaspoon salt
> Dash to 1/8 teaspoon ground cinnamon

**1.** In a large bowl, dissolve gelatin in boiling water. Stir in cold water. Cover and refrigerate until partially set, about 1-1/2 hours. Fold in the apples, celery and walnuts. Pour into a 6-cup ring mold coated with cooking spray. Cover and refrigerate for 4 hours or until set.

**2.** For dressing, combine the yogurt, brown sugar, salt and cinnamon; chill until serving. To serve, unmold salad onto a platter. Serve with dressing. **Yield:** 12 servings.

# Meatball Sandwiches

*These moist and tender meatball sandwiches are perfect when you're hosting a holiday open house or progressive dinner. Keep the meatballs warm in a slow cooker, and let guests serve themselves as they arrive.* ~Ruby Steigleder, Selma, California

    1 egg, lightly beaten
    1/2 cup milk
    1/2 cup dry bread crumbs
    1/4 cup finely chopped onion
    1/2 teaspoon salt
    1/4 teaspoon garlic powder
    1/4 teaspoon pepper
    1-1/2 pounds ground beef
    BARBECUE SAUCE:
        1 large onion, chopped
        2 garlic cloves, minced
        2 tablespoons canola oil
        3 cups water
        1 can (12 ounces) tomato paste
        2 teaspoons salt
        1 teaspoon sugar
        1 teaspoon dried oregano
        1/4 teaspoon pepper
        1 bay leaf
    14 submarine buns (6 inches *each*), split
    1-3/4 cups shredded part-skim mozzarella cheese

**1.** In a large bowl, combine the egg, milk, bread crumbs, onion, salt, garlic powder and pepper. Crumble beef over mixture and mix well. Shape into 1-1/2-in. balls. Place on a greased rack in a shallow baking pan. Bake, uncovered, at 350° for 30-35 minutes or until no longer pink. Drain on paper towels.

**2.** Meanwhile, for sauce, in a Dutch oven, saute onion and garlic in oil for 3-4 minutes or until tender. Stir in the water, tomato paste, salt, sugar, oregano, pepper and bay leaf. Bring to a boil. Add the meatballs. Reduce heat; simmer, uncovered, for 10-15 minutes or until heated through.

**3.** Discard bay leaf. Spoon five meatballs with sauce onto each bun bottom. Sprinkle with cheese. Replace tops. **Yield:** 14 servings.

# Whipped Orange Sweet Potatoes

*Skip your usual potato recipes and add excitement to the table with this whipped sensation. It features the tang of orange and the crunch of pecans.* ~Doris Strom, Renton, Washington

    2 pounds medium sweet potatoes, cooked, peeled
        and cubed
    1 egg
    1/4 cup packed brown sugar
    1/4 cup orange juice
    2 tablespoons butter
    2 tablespoons sour cream
    1 teaspoon grated orange peel
    1/2 teaspoon ground cinnamon
    1/4 cup chopped pecans

*Whipped Orange Sweet Potatoes*

In a large bowl, beat potatoes until smooth. Beat in the egg, brown sugar, orange juice, butter, sour cream, orange peel and cinnamon. Pour into a greased 1-1/2-qt. baking dish. Sprinkle with pecans. Bake, uncovered, at 350° for 25-30 minutes or until a thermometer reads 160°. **Yield:** 7 servings.

# Wild Rice Turkey Soup

*This soup is guaranteed to chase away the chills on cold winter nights. The smooth, rich, not-too-thick broth has the earthy flavor of wild rice and Worcestershire sauce. Your family and friends will love the creamy texture and unique taste.*
~Val Lefebvre, Rosetown, Saskatchewan

    6 cups chicken broth, *divided*
    2 cups sliced fresh mushrooms
    2 medium onions, chopped
    2 medium carrots, shredded
    1/2 cup uncooked wild rice
    4 garlic cloves, minced
    6 tablespoons butter, cubed
    1/2 cup all-purpose flour
    1 teaspoon salt
    1/2 teaspoon pepper
    4 cups milk
    2 cups cubed cooked turkey
    2 to 3 teaspoons Worcestershire sauce
    1/4 cup minced fresh parsley

**1.** In a soup kettle, combine 3 cups broth, mushrooms, onions, carrots, rice and garlic; bring to a boil. Reduce heat; cover and simmer for 50-55 minutes or until rice is tender.

**2.** In a large saucepan, melt butter over medium heat. Whisk in the flour, salt and pepper until smooth. Gradually whisk in milk and the remaining broth. Bring to a boil. Cook and stir for 2 minutes or until thickened. Add to rice mixture. Add turkey and Worcestershire sauce; heat through. Garnish with parsley. **Yield:** 9 servings (3-1/2 quarts).

*Triple-Layer Chocolate Cake*

# Delightful Desserts

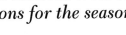

Christmastime menus just aren't complete without a luscious treat to top it all off. You'll find a wide assortment of sweet creations for the season here.

## Triple-Layer Chocolate Cake

*Pecans and coconut fill each luscious layer of this tempting cake topped with a homemade frosting. Big slices are guaranteed to make eyes light up!* ~Abigail Rider, East Point, Kentucky

    1/2 cup butter, softened
    1/2 cup shortening
      2 cups sugar
      5 eggs
      1 teaspoon vanilla extract
      2 cups all-purpose flour
    1/4 cup baking cocoa
      1 teaspoon baking soda
      1 cup buttermilk
      1 cup flaked coconut
      1 cup chopped pecans
CHOCOLATE CREAM CHEESE FROSTING:
      1 package (8 ounces) cream cheese, softened
    1/2 cup butter, softened
      4 cups confectioners' sugar
    1/4 cup baking cocoa
      1 teaspoon vanilla extract
Pinch salt

**1.** In a large bowl, cream the butter, shortening and sugar until light and fluffy. Add eggs, one at a time, beating well after each addition. Stir in vanilla. Combine the flour, cocoa and baking soda; add to the creamed mixture alternately with buttermilk. Fold in coconut and pecans.

**2.** Pour into three greased and floured 9-in. round baking pans. Bake at 350° for 20-25 minutes or until a toothpick inserted near the center comes out clean. Cool for 10 minutes before removing from pans to wire racks to cool completely.

**3.** In a large bowl, beat cream cheese and butter until fluffy. Add the confectioners' sugar, cocoa, vanilla and salt; beat until smooth. Spread frosting between layers and over top and sides of cake. Store in the refrigerator. **Yield:** 12 servings.

## Gingerbread Cupcakes

*The robust ginger flavor of these cakes is mellowed by the creamy maple frosting's sweetness. For an extra-special touch, add candied ginger as a garnish.* ~Nancy Beckman, Helena, Montana

    1/2 cup butter, softened
    1/2 cup packed brown sugar
      1 egg
    1/2 cup water
    1/2 cup molasses

    1-1/3 cups all-purpose flour
      3/4 teaspoon ground cinnamon
      1/2 teaspoon baking powder
      1/2 teaspoon baking soda
      1/2 teaspoon salt
      1/2 teaspoon ground ginger
      1/2 teaspoon ground nutmeg
      1/4 teaspoon ground allspice
MAPLE FROSTING:
      1/3 cup butter, softened
        1 ounce cream cheese, softened
      1/4 cup packed brown sugar
Dash salt
      1/4 cup maple syrup
      1/4 teaspoon vanilla extract
        1 cup confectioners' sugar

**1.** In a large bowl, cream butter and brown sugar until light and fluffy. Add egg; beat well. Stir in water and molasses. Combine the flour, cinnamon, baking powder, baking soda, salt, ginger, nutmeg and allspice. Add to the creamed mixture; beat on low speed until combined. Beat on medium for 2 minutes.

**2.** Fill paper-lined muffin cups two-thirds full. Bake at 350° for 20-25 minutes or until a toothpick comes out clean. Cool for 10 minutes before removing to a wire rack to cool completely.

**3.** For frosting, in a small bowl, cream the butter, cream cheese, brown sugar and salt until fluffy. Add maple syrup and vanilla. Gradually beat in confectioners' sugar until smooth. Frost cupcakes. Store in the refrigerator. **Yield:** 1 dozen.

*Gingerbread Cupcakes*

# Cran-Raspberry Pie

*With ruby-red fruit and a lattice crust, this home-style pie is perfect for a Christmas table. The sweet-tart berries are accented with a hint of almond.* ~Vivian Gallagher, Berlin, New Jersey

   2-1/4 cups all-purpose flour
      1 tablespoon sugar
      1 teaspoon salt
    3/4 cup shortening
      1 egg yolk, beaten
      4 to 5 tablespoons cold water
      1 teaspoon almond extract
FILLING:
   2-1/4 cups fresh *or* frozen cranberries, thawed and
      coarsely chopped
   2-1/4 cups fresh *or* frozen raspberries
   1-1/4 cups plus 1 tablespoon sugar, *divided*
      2 tablespoons quick-cooking tapioca
    1/4 teaspoon almond extract
      2 tablespoons butter
      1 egg white, lightly beaten

**1.** In a large bowl, combine the flour, sugar and salt; cut in shortening until crumbly. In a small bowl, combine the egg yolk, cold water and almond extract; gradually add to flour mixture, tossing with a fork until dough forms a ball.

**2.** Divide dough in half so that one ball is slightly larger than the other. On a lightly floured surface, roll out larger ball to fit a 9-in. pie plate. Transfer pastry to pie plate; trim even with edge of plate.

**3.** In a large bowl, combine the cranberries, raspberries, 1-1/4 cups sugar, tapioca and extract; stir gently and let stand for 15 minutes. Spoon filling into crust; dot with butter. Roll out remaining pastry; make a lattice crust. Trim, seal and flute edges. Brush with egg white; sprinkle with remaining sugar.

**4.** Bake at 425° for 15 minutes. Reduce heat to 350°; bake 30-35 minutes longer or until crust is golden brown and the filling is bubbly. Cool completely on a wire rack. Refrigerate until serving. **Yield:** 8 servings.

# Persimmon Pudding

*When a group of ladies and I served this cake-like dessert for a church get-together, it was an immediate success. The persimmon flavor is subtle, and the butter sauce adds elegance.*
~Viola Darrow, Klamath Falls, Oregon

      2 tablespoons butter
      1 cup sugar
      1 egg
      1 cup all-purpose flour
      2 teaspoons baking soda
    1/2 teaspoon salt
    1/4 teaspoon ground cinnamon
    1/2 cup milk
      1 cup mashed ripe persimmon pulp (about
      3 medium)
BUTTER SAUCE:
      1 cup sugar
    1/2 cup evaporated milk
      1 tablespoon butter
Dash salt
 1-1/2 teaspoons vanilla extract

**1.** In a large bowl, cream butter and sugar until crumbly, about 2 minutes. Add egg; beat well. Combine the flour, baking soda, salt and cinnamon; add to the creamed mixture alternately with milk. Stir in persimmon pulp.

**2.** Pour into six well-greased 8-oz. custard cups or ramekins. Cover tightly with a double layer of foil. Place on a rack in a deep kettle. Add 1 in. of boiling water to kettle; cover and boil gently. Replace water as needed. Steam for 1-1/2 hours or until a toothpick inserted near the center comes out clean. Let stand 10 minutes before removing from custard cups.

**3.** For the butter sauce, in a small saucepan, combine the sugar, evaporated milk, butter and salt. Cook and stir over medium heat for 3-5 minutes or until heated through. Remove from the heat; stir in vanilla. Drizzle over the pudding. **Yield:** 6 servings.

**Editor's Note:** Use the Hachiya, acorn-shaped, variety persimmon that is ripe and soft. To scoop out Hachiya persimmon for mashing or pureeing, halve the fruit and scoop out the pulp with a spoon, discarding the stem, skin and seeds, if any.

# Banana Cream Meringue Pie

*I grew up on a farm in Alberta, and I still remember my mom's pies, fresh from the oven for suppertime. This creamy banana variety is so good. No store-bought version can compare!*
~Carol Maertz, Spruce Grove, Alberta

Pastry for single-crust pie (9 inches)
      1 cup sugar, *divided*

*Cran-Raspberry Pie*

1/3 cup cornstarch
1/2 teaspoon salt
1 can (12 ounces) evaporated milk
1 cup water
3 egg yolks, lightly beaten
1 teaspoon vanilla extract
3 egg whites
1 large firm banana

1. Line a 9-in. pie plate with pastry; trim and flute edges. Line pastry shell with a double thickness of heavy-duty foil. Bake at 450° for 8 minutes. Remove foil; bake 5 minutes longer. Cool on a wire rack.

2. In a large saucepan, combine 2/3 cup sugar, cornstarch and salt. Stir in milk and water until smooth. Cook and stir over medium-high heat until thickened and bubbly. Reduce heat; cook and stir 2 minutes longer. Remove from the heat. Stir a small amount of hot filling into egg yolks; return all to pan, stirring constantly. Bring to a gentle boil; cook and stir 2 minutes longer. Remove from the heat. Gently stir in vanilla. Keep warm.

3. In a large bowl, beat egg whites on medium speed until soft peaks form. Gradually beat in remaining sugar, 1 tablespoon at a time, on high until stiff glossy peaks form and sugar is dissolved. Slice banana into crust; pour filling over top. Spread meringue evenly over hot filling, sealing edges to crust.

4. Bake at 350° for 12-15 minutes or until golden brown. Cool on a wire rack for 1 hour. Refrigerate for at least 3 hours before serving. **Yield:** 8 servings.

*Toffee Almond Tart*

2. Pour into a greased 13-in. x 9-in. baking dish. Bake at 350° for 30-35 minutes or until a toothpick inserted near the center comes out with moist crumbs (do not over bake). Cool on a wire rack.

3. In a large bowl, beat cream cheese and 1/2 cup milk until smooth. Add pudding mix and remaining milk; beat for 2 minutes or until thickened. Stir in extract; fold in whipped topping. Spread over cooled brownies. Refrigerate until set.

4. Just before serving, drizzle with caramel topping and garnish with chocolate curls if desired. **Yield:** 2-1/2 dozen.

# Snowcapped Brownies

(Pictured on page 59)

*Baking is one of my hobbies, and my wife says these brownies topped with a cream cheese layer are great. When you really want to impress, drizzle them with caramel sauce and add chocolate curls.* ~Lyle Borcherding, Johnstown, Pennsylvania

1 cup butter, cubed
3/4 cup baking cocoa
4 eggs
2 cups sugar
1 teaspoon vanilla extract
1 cup all-purpose flour
1/2 teaspoon salt
2 cups (12 ounces) semisweet chocolate chips
1 cup chopped nuts, optional
TOPPING:
4 ounces cream cheese, softened
1-1/2 cups cold milk, *divided*
1 package (3.4 ounces) instant vanilla pudding mix
1/8 teaspoon almond extract
1-1/2 cups whipped topping
Caramel ice cream topping and chocolate curls, optional

1. In a small saucepan, melt butter; stir in cocoa until smooth. Remove from the heat. In a large bowl, beat the eggs, sugar and vanilla for 1 minute. Gradually add flour and salt. Stir in cocoa mixture. Fold in chocolate chips and nuts if desired.

# Toffee Almond Tart

*My aunt gave this recipe to my mother, who shared it with me. Both of them are terrific cooks, so I knew it had to be a winner. I wasn't disappointed!* ~Sharlyn Nichols, Livingston, California

2 cups all-purpose flour
3 tablespoons plus 1-1/2 cups sugar, *divided*
3/4 cup cold butter, cubed
3 egg yolks
1-1/2 cups heavy whipping cream
1/4 teaspoon salt
2 cups sliced almonds
1 teaspoon vanilla extract

1. In a large bowl, combine flour and 3 tablespoons sugar; cut in butter until mixture resembles fine crumbs. Add egg yolks, tossing with a fork until combined.

2. Press onto the bottom and up the sides of an ungreased 11-in. fluted tart pan with removable bottom. Place pan on a baking sheet. Bake at 375° for 10 minutes or until golden brown.

3. Meanwhile, in a large saucepan, combine the cream, salt and remaining sugar. Bring to a boil over medium heat, stirring constantly. Remove from the heat; stir in almonds and vanilla. Pour into crust.

4. Bake for 30-35 minutes or until golden brown. Cool on a wire rack. Store in the refrigerator. **Yield:** 14 servings.

*Snap Dessert Cups*

## Snap Dessert Cups

*For that "wow" factor, it's hard to top these extra-special treats. The homemade cranberry ice cream is served in edible brandy-flavored cups and covered with a decadent caramel sauce.*
*~Karen Rubin, Raymond, New Hampshire*

 3 cups heavy whipping cream
 1 cup sugar
 1 package (12 ounces) fresh cranberries
 1/4 cup water
BRANDY SNAP CUPS:
 1/2 cup butter, cubed
 1/2 cup sugar
 1/3 cup molasses
 1 teaspoon grated orange peel
 1/2 teaspoon ground cinnamon
 1/4 teaspoon ground ginger
 1/4 cup all-purpose flour
 1 teaspoon brandy extract
CARAMEL SAUCE:
 1/2 cup butter, cubed
 1/4 cup water
 1 cup sugar
 1 cup heavy whipping cream
 1 teaspoon vanilla extract

**1.** In a large heavy saucepan, combine cream and sugar. Cook and stir over medium heat until sugar is dissolved; set aside. In a small saucepan, combine cranberries and water. Cook over medium heat until the berries pop, about 15 minutes.

**2.** Press cranberry mixture through a sieve; discard skins and seeds. In a large bowl, combine cranberry pulp and cream mixture; mix well. Cover and refrigerate until chilled.

**3.** Fill cylinder of ice cream freezer two-thirds full; freeze according to the manufacturer's directions. Refrigerate remaining mixture until ready to freeze. When ice cream is frozen, transfer to a freezer container; freeze for 2-4 hours before serving.

**4.** In a large saucepan, combine the butter, sugar, molasses, orange peel, cinnamon and ginger. Bring to a boil. Remove from the heat. Quickly whisk in flour and extract until smooth. Place pan over a pan of boiling water to hold mixture at a spoonable consistency.

**5.** Prepare only two brandy snap cups at a time. Spoon 1 tablespoon of molasses mixture onto opposite ends of a greased baking sheet, forming two circles. Bake at 300° for 10 minutes or until bubbly and deep golden brown. Cool on pan on wire rack for 2 minutes.

**6.** Quickly loosen one at a time, and place each over an inverted greased 8-oz. custard cup, carefully shaping to the custard cup. Cool for 5 minutes. Carefully remove from custard cups. Repeat five times.

**7.** For sauce, combine butter and water in a heavy saucepan. Cook and stir over medium-low heat until butter is melted; add sugar. Cook and stir until sugar is dissolved. Bring to a boil without stirring over medium-high heat. Boil and stir for 4 minutes longer or until mixture turns deep amber. Remove from the heat. Carefully stir in cream and vanilla.

**8.** To assemble, serve cranberry ice cream in brandy snap cups. Drizzle with caramel sauce. **Yield:** 10 servings.

## Frozen Cranberry Pie With Candied Almonds

*It's so convenient to fix part of a holiday feast in advance. This ginger-spiced delight goes in the freezer overnight and is ready to enjoy the next day.* *~Rosemary Johnson, Irondale, Alabama*

 24 gingersnap cookies
 3/4 cup milk
 2 packages (3.4 ounces *each*) instant French vanilla pudding mix
 1 can (16 ounces) whole-berry cranberry sauce
 1 carton (8 ounces) frozen French vanilla whipped topping, thawed, *divided*
 1/2 cup slivered almonds, *divided*
 1 teaspoon candied *or* crystallized ginger, chopped
 1 teaspoon almond extract
 2 teaspoons butter
 2 tablespoons brown sugar

**1.** Arrange cookies around the bottom and up the sides of an ungreased 9-in. pie plate, cutting cookies if necessary to fit.

**2.** In a small bowl, combine milk and pudding mixes. Stir in cranberry sauce, 1/2 cup whipped topping, 1/3 cup almonds, ginger and extract. Pour into prepared plate; chill for 1 hour.

**3.** Meanwhile, in a small heavy skillet, melt butter. Add remaining almonds; cook over medium heat until nuts are toasted, about 4 minutes. Sprinkle with sugar. Cook and stir for 2-4 minutes or until sugar is melted. Spread on foil to cool.

**4.** Spread remaining whipped topping over filling; sprinkle with almonds. Cover and freeze overnight. **Yield:** 8 servings.

*Snowcapped Brownies (p. 57)*
*Frozen Cranberry Pie with Candied Almonds*

*Tarragon Vinegar*
*Dixie Herb Rub* (p. 62)

# Gifts from the Kitchen

⋆ *Warm the hearts of everyone on your list this Christmas with scrumptious, tasteful treats made at home. Store-bought varieties just can't compare!* ⋆

## Tarragon Vinegar

*Add fresh tarragon sprigs to basic white wine vinegar in a decorative bottle, and you'll have an elegant Christmas present for family or friends who love to cook. If you like, include recipes for salad dressing or other foods that could use this distinctive blend.* ~Sue Gronholz, Beaver Dam, Wisconsin

  1 cup tarragon sprigs
  2 cups white wine vinegar
Additional fresh tarragon sprig, optional

1. Wash tarragon and pat dry. Place in a sterilized jar. Using a wooden spoon, gently bruise the tarragon. Add the vinegar. Cover and store in a cool dark place for 2-3 weeks to let flavors develop.

2. Strain and discard the tarragon. Pour the tarragon vinegar into a sterilized decorative bottle. Add additional tarragon if desired. Store vinegar in a cool dark place for up to 6 months. **Yield:** 2 cups.

## Spiced Pecans

*You may want to make more than one batch of these nuts spiced with coriander, cinnamon, nutmeg and allspice. They disappear fast! Pack some in gift tins but keep some at home to offer your guests, too.* ~Michelle Krzmarzick, Redondo Beach, California

  1/2 cup sugar
  3 tablespoons butter, melted
  1 tablespoon light corn syrup
  1 tablespoon vanilla extract
  6 cups water
  1 pound pecan halves
  1/4 teaspoon salt
  1/4 teaspoon *each* ground coriander, cinnamon,
    nutmeg and allspice
  1/8 teaspoon pepper

1. In a large bowl, combine the sugar, butter, corn syrup and vanilla; set aside. In a large saucepan, combine water and pecans; bring to a boil for 1 minute. Drain. Immediately add to sugar mixture; toss to coat.

2. Transfer to an ungreased 15-in. x 10-in. baking sheet. Bake at 325° for 30-35 minutes or until browned, stirring every 10 minutes.

3. Combine the remaining ingredients; sprinkle over the hot pecans. Stir to coat. Spread pecans in a single layer on a baking sheet; cool on a wire rack. Store in an airtight container. **Yield:** 5 cups.

## Crunchy Granola

*This mix is ideal for anyone who appreciates yummy but wholesome snacks. Honey, brown sugar and molasses add just the right amount of sweetness.* ~Sandy Vennink, Manilla, Iowa

  2 cartons (18 ounces *each*) old-fashioned oats
  2 cups Grape-Nuts
1-1/2 cups flaked coconut
  1 cup toasted wheat germ
  1 cup sunflower kernels
  1 cup chopped almonds
  1 cup chopped walnuts
1/2 cup sesame seeds
  1 cup packed brown sugar
  1 cup butter, cubed
  1 cup honey
1/2 cup canola oil
  2 tablespoons molasses
  3 teaspoons vanilla extract
1/2 teaspoon salt
  3 cups raisins

1. In a very large bowl, combine the first eight ingredients. In a large saucepan over medium heat, cook the brown sugar, butter, honey, oil and molasses for 2-3 minutes or until sugar is dissolved. Remove from the heat; stir in vanilla and salt. Pour over oat mixture and toss to coat.

2. Transfer to two greased 15-in. x 10-in. baking pans. Bake at 350° for 20-25 minutes or until golden brown, stirring twice. Cool, stirring occasionally. Stir in raisins. Store in airtight containers. **Yield:** 6-1/2 quarts.

*Crunchy Granola*
*Spiced Pecans*

# Mint Chocolate Sauce

*This thick, rich sauce reminds everyone of after-dinner mints. Pour it over vanilla ice cream or pound cake to instantly create a decadent dessert.* ~Marlene Wiczek, Little Falls, Minnesota

    2 cups sugar
    1 cup butter, cubed
    1/2 cup water
    1/2 cup light corn syrup
    4 cups (24 ounces) semisweet chocolate chips
    1/2 cup creme de menthe
Ice cream

**1.** In a large saucepan, combine the sugar, butter, water and corn syrup. Bring to a boil over medium heat, stirring constantly. Boil for 3 minutes. Remove from the heat. Add chocolate chips and creme de menthe; whisk until smooth.

**2.** Serve warm over ice cream or transfer to storage containers and refrigerate.

**3. To serve:** Scoop out desired quantity and reheat in microwave until warmed. **Yield:** about 5 cups.

# Crispy Chip Candy Mix

*My kids and grandkids like to help me assemble this no-bake treat. The mix looks pretty in a jar and speeds up the process of making yummy candies.* ~Edie DeSpain, Logan, Utah

    3/4 cup flaked coconut
    1-1/2 cups crisp rice cereal
    3/4 cup miniature semisweet chocolate chips
    1 cup confectioners' sugar
    1/4 cup chopped pecans, toasted
    1/2 cup dried cherries

*Crispy Chip Candy Mix*

**ADDITIONAL INGREDIENTS:**
    1 cup creamy peanut butter
    1/4 cup butter, softened

**1.** Place coconut in a small resealable plastic bag; set aside. In a 1-qt. jar with a tight-fitting lid, layer the cereal, chocolate chips, confectioners' sugar, pecans and cherries. Place bag in jar. Cover and store in a cool dry place for up to 6 months.

**2. To prepare candy:** In a large bowl, combine peanut butter and butter. Stir in candy mix and mix well. Shape into 1-in. balls; roll in coconut. Refrigerate at least 2 hours. Store in the refrigerator. **Yield:** about 2-1/2 dozen.

**Editor's Note:** Reduced-fat or generic brands of peanut butter are not recommended for this recipe.

# Dixie Herb Rub

(Pictured on page 60)

*This flavorful blend is a mouth-watering way to season poultry, beef or pork. My husband loves it when I use this rub to jazz up a chicken dinner.* ~Traci Wynne, Clayton, Delaware

    1 tablespoon *each* dried basil, thyme and rosemary,
        crushed
    1-1/2 teaspoons sugar
    1-1/2 teaspoons dried oregano
    1-1/2 teaspoons dried marjoram
    1 teaspoon salt
    3/4 teaspoon garlic powder
    1/2 teaspoon pepper
    1/4 teaspoon onion powder
    1/4 teaspoon cayenne pepper

In a bowl, combine all ingredients. Store in a covered container. Rub over poultry or meat before grilling, baking or broiling. **Yield:** 1/3 cup.

# Mocha Cashew Butter

*Here's a yummy alternative to the usual peanut butter. With chocolate and coffee accenting the nuts, this spread turns ordinary toast, muffins and more into scrumptious delights.* ~Mary Houchin, Swansea, Illinois

    3 cups salted cashews
    1/2 cup butter, softened, *divided*
    1/2 cup semisweet chocolate chips
    2 teaspoons instant coffee granules
    2 teaspoons water
Additional salted cashews, optional

**1.** Place cashews in a food processor. Cover and process until finely ground. Add half of the butter; process until smooth. Transfer to a small bowl.

**2.** In a small saucepan, combine the chocolate chips, coffee granules, water and remaining butter. Cook and stir over low heat until smooth. Stir into the cashew mixture. Top with additional cashews if desired. Store in the refrigerator. **Yield:** 2-1/4 cups.

# Citrus Nut Biscotti

*I lived in Italy for over seven years and started every morning meal with biscotti. This version features the flavors of orange and lemon.*  ~Cindy Harris, San Antonio, Texas

    1/2 cup butter, softened
      1 cup sugar
      3 eggs
      1 teaspoon *each* almond, rum and vanilla extract
      3 cups all-purpose flour
1-1/2 teaspoons baking powder
    1/8 teaspoon salt
      1 cup chopped walnuts, toasted
      4 teaspoons grated lemon peel
      4 teaspoons grated orange peel

**1.** In a large bowl, cream butter and sugar. Beat in eggs and extracts. Combine flour, baking powder and salt; gradually add to creamed mixture and mix well. Stir in walnuts and peel.

**2.** Divide dough in half. On a greased baking sheet, shape each half into an 11-in. x 3-in. rectangle. Bake at 350° for 20-25 minutes or until golden brown and firm to the touch.

**3.** Carefully remove to wire racks; cool for 15 minutes. Transfer to a cutting board; cut diagonally with a serrated knife into 1/2-in. slices. Place slices cut side down on ungreased baking sheets. Bake for 10 minutes on each side. Remove to wire racks to cool. Store in an airtight container. **Yield:** about 3 dozen.

# Lemony Poppy Seed Muffins

*These citrusy goodies are always popular at brunches. For a gift, pack the muffins in a festive basket with a jar of your favorite jam or preserves.*  ~Kimberly Baxter, Exeter, Rhode Island

    1/2 cup butter, softened
    3/4 cup sugar
      2 eggs

*Lemony Poppy Seed Muffins*

    3/4 cup sour cream
    1/4 cup lemon juice
      3 teaspoons lemon extract
      1 teaspoon vanilla extract
      1 teaspoon grated lemon peel
      2 cups all-purpose flour
      1 teaspoon baking powder
      1 teaspoon baking soda
    1/4 teaspoon salt
      2 tablespoons poppy seeds

**1.** In a large bowl, cream butter and sugar until light and fluffy. Add eggs, one at a time, beating well after each addition. Stir in the sour cream, lemon juice, extracts and peel.

**2.** Combine the flour, baking powder, baking soda and salt; add to creamed mixture just until moistened. Fold in poppy seeds. Fill six greased jumbo muffin pans.

**3.** Bake at 375° for 20-23 minutes or until a toothpick comes out clean. Remove to a wire rack. **Yield:** 6 jumbo muffins.

# Dog Biscuits

*Like to give Christmas gifts to friends of the canine kind? Treat them to these homemade biscuits flavored with peanut butter and formed with a bone-shaped cookie cutter. (See page 91 to find out how to make the cute doggie gift package shown in the photo at far right.)*
~Ryan Nicholas, Pewaukee, Wisconsin

    2 cups whole wheat flour
    1 cup toasted wheat germ
  1/2 teaspoon salt
    1 cup creamy peanut butter
  1/2 cup water
    1 egg
  1/4 cup canola oil

**1.** In a large bowl, combine the wheat flour, wheat germ and salt. Stir in the peanut butter, water, egg and oil. On a floured surface, roll dough to 1/2-in. thickness. Cut with a 3-in. bone-shaped cookie cutter.

**2.** Place 2-in. apart on ungreased baking sheets. Bake at 350° for 18-23 minutes or until the bottoms are lightly browned (tops may crack). Cool on a wire rack. Store in an airtight container. **Yield:** 32 dog biscuits.

**Editor's Note:** Reduced-fat or generic brands of peanut butter are not recommended for this recipe.

For: Hootie

Best Butter Cookies

# Cookie Confections

Fill your holiday gift tins, Christmas cookie trays and a plate for Santa, too with everything from festively frosted cutouts to old-world Italian delights.

## Best Butter Cookies

*With this convenient recipe, you get four kinds of cookies from just one batch of dough—cutouts, peppermint balls, fruit balls and chocolate slices.* ~Dawn Fagerstrom, Warren, Minnesota

2 cups butter, softened
1-1/2 cups sugar
2 eggs
1 teaspoon vanilla extract
5 cups all-purpose flour
2 teaspoons baking powder
1/4 teaspoon salt

ADDITIONAL INGREDIENTS FOR CUTOUTS:
Sprinkles, jimmies *or* colored sugar, optional

ADDITIONAL INGREDIENTS FOR PEPPERMINT BALLS:
1/4 cup crushed peppermint candies
1/4 teaspoon peppermint extract
Red colored sugar, optional

ADDITIONAL INGREDIENTS FOR SPICY FRUIT BALLS:
1/2 cup dried currants
1/2 cup chopped mixed candied fruit
1/2 teaspoon ground cinnamon
Confectioners' sugar, optional

ADDITIONAL INGREDIENTS FOR CHOCOLATE SLICES:
1 square (1 ounce) unsweetened chocolate
1/2 cup chopped pecans

**1.** In a large bowl, cream butter and sugar until light and fluffy. Beat in eggs and vanilla. Combine flour, baking powder and salt; gradually add to creamed mixture and mix well.

**2.** Divide dough into four 1-1/2 cup portions; mix and shape for each variety as follows. **Yield:** 4 portions (1-1/2 cups each).

**3. To prepare Cutouts:** Using one portion dough, divide into two balls; roll each ball directly on an ungreased baking sheet to 1/8-in. thickness. Cut with a floured cookie cutter, leaving at least 1 in. between cookies. Remove excess dough and reroll scraps if desired. Decorate with sprinkles, jimmies or colored sugar if desired. Bake at 375° for 6-7 minutes or until edges begin to brown. Cool for 1 minute before removing from pans to wire racks. **Yield:** 2 dozen.

**4. To prepare Peppermint Balls:** In a large bowl, combine one portion dough, peppermint candies and peppermint extract. Shape into 1-in. balls; place 2 in. apart on ungreased baking sheets. Sprinkle with red colored sugar if desired. Bake at 375° for 10-12 minutes or until set. Cool for 1 minute before removing from pans to wire racks. **Yield:** 2 dozen.

**5. To prepare Spicy Fruit Balls:** In a large bowl, combine one portion dough, currants, fruit and cinnamon. Shape into 1-in. balls; place 2 in. apart on ungreased baking sheets. Bake at 375° for 10-12 minutes or until set. Cool for 1 minute, then roll in confectioners' sugar if desired. Cool on wire racks. **Yield:** 2 dozen.

**6. To prepare Chocolate Slices:** In a microwave, melt chocolate; stir until smooth. In a small bowl, mix melted chocolate into one portion cookie dough. Shape into a 1-1/2-in.-thick log; roll in nuts. Wrap in plastic wrap and refrigerate for 4 hours or until firm. Unwrap and cut into 1/8-in. slices. Place 2 in. apart on ungreased baking sheets. Bake at 375° for 8-10 minutes or until set. Cool for 1 minute before removing from pans to wire racks. **Yield:** 3 dozen.

## Peppermint Puff Pastry Sticks

*I wanted to impress my husband's family with something you might expect to find in a European bakery, and these are what I came up with.* ~Darlene Brenden, Salem, Oregon

1 sheet frozen puff pastry, thawed
10 ounces chocolate almond bark, coarsely chopped
1-1/2 cups crushed peppermint candies

**1.** Unfold pastry sheet onto a lightly floured surface. Cut into 4-in. x 1/2-in. strips. Place on greased baking sheets. Bake at 400° for 12-15 minutes or until golden brown. Remove to wire racks to cool.

**2.** In a microwave-safe bowl, melt almond bark; stir until smooth. Dip each cookie halfway, allowing excess to drip off. Sprinkle with candies. Place on waxed paper; let stand until set. Store in an airtight container. **Yield:** about 3 dozen.

*Peppermint Puff Pastry Sticks*

# Citrus Almond Cookies

*In my mother's family, these little frosted rounds were a "must" every Christmas. And I was surprised Mom consented to let me share the secret recipe! We think the blend of toasted almonds, milk chocolate, orange and lemon is cookie perfection.*
*~Cherie Donohue, Happy Valley, Oregon*

   4 cups unblanched almonds, toasted
   1 cup sugar
   5 milk chocolate candy bars (1.55 ounces *each*), chopped
   1/2 teaspoon ground cinnamon
   2 eggs
   4 teaspoons grated orange peel
   1 tablespoon orange juice
   2 teaspoons grated lemon peel
   2 teaspoons vanilla extract
   1 teaspoon lemon extract
FROSTING:
   1 cup confectioners' sugar
   1/2 teaspoon lemon extract
   1/2 teaspoon vanilla extract
   2 to 4 teaspoons water

**1.** Place almonds in a food processor; cover and process until chopped. In a large bowl, combine the almonds, sugar, chocolate and cinnamon; set aside.

**2.** In a small bowl, beat the eggs, orange peel, orange juice, lemon peel and extracts until combined. Gradually add to almond mixture and mix well. Cover and refrigerate for 2 hours or until easy to handle.

**3.** Roll the cookie dough into 1-in. balls. Place the balls 2 in. apart on parchment paper-lined baking sheets. Bake at 325°

for 12-15 minutes or until bottoms are lightly browned. Remove to wire racks to cool.

**4.** Meanwhile, in a small bowl, combine the confectioners' sugar, extracts and enough water to achieve spreading consistency. Spread over cooled cookies. Store in airtight containers. **Yield:** 6 dozen.

# Acorn Shortbread Cookies

*These buttery treats are just as fun to make as they are to eat. Shaped like acorns, the cookies are dipped into melted chocolate to create the "caps" and then sprinkled with chopped pecans. They're popular during autumn and all winter long.*
*~Margie Williams, Mt. Juliet, Tennessee*

   1 cup butter, softened
   3/4 cup packed brown sugar
   1 teaspoon vanilla extract
2-1/2 cups all-purpose flour
   1/2 teaspoon baking powder
   3/4 cup finely chopped pecans, *divided*
   1 cup (6 ounces) semisweet chocolate chips
   1 tablespoon shortening

**1.** In a large bowl, cream butter and brown sugar until light and fluffy. Beat in vanilla. Combine flour and baking powder; gradually add to creamed mixture and mix well. Stir in 1/3 cup pecans.

**2.** Shape tablespoonfuls of dough into acorn shapes, pinching bottoms to form a point. Place 2 in. apart on ungreased baking sheets. Bake at 350° for 8-10 minutes or until set. Remove to wire racks to cool.

**3.** In a microwave, melt chocolate chips and shortening; stir until smooth. Dip the top of each cookie in chocolate mixture, allowing excess to drip off. Immediately sprinkle remaining pecans over chocolate. Place on waxed paper; let stand until set. **Yield:** 3-1/2 dozen.

# Glazed Italian Spice Cookies

*Like to have a wide variety of treats on your Christmas cookie tray? These cute balls give you a soft, cake-like option—a nice complement to your crispy and crunchy offerings. The creamy almond glaze spread on top makes them extra yummy.*
*~Shelia Hake, Bossier City, Louisiana*

   1 cup shortening
1-1/4 cups sugar
   3 eggs
   1 cup milk
   5 cups all-purpose flour
   1/4 cup plus 3 tablespoons baking cocoa
   5 teaspoons baking powder
   1 teaspoon ground cinnamon
   1 teaspoon ground nutmeg
   1/2 teaspoon ground cloves
   1/4 teaspoon baking soda
   1 cup finely chopped pecans

*Citrus Almond Cookies*

GLAZE:
     6 tablespoons butter, softened
2-1/2 cups confectioners' sugar
     3 tablespoons milk
     1 teaspoon vanilla extract
     1/4 teaspoon almond extract

**1.** In a large bowl, cream shortening and sugar until light and fluffy. Beat in eggs and milk. Combine the flour, cocoa, baking powder, cinnamon, nutmeg, cloves and baking soda; gradually add to creamed mixture and mix well. Stir in pecans.

**2.** Roll dough into 1-in. balls. Place 1 in. apart on greased baking sheets. Bake at 350° for 9-11 minutes or until edges are set. Remove to wire racks to cool.

**3.** For glaze, in a large bowl, beat butter until fluffy. Add the confectioners' sugar, milk and extracts; beat until smooth. Spread over cooled cookies. **Yield:** 7-1/2 dozen.

## Almond Espresso Bars

*If you're a coffee lover, you're sure to like these mocha morsels made with espresso and dressed up with almonds. You'll want to save some for snacktime and even breakfast, too.*
~Taire Van Scoy, Brunswick, Maryland

     1/4 cup butter, softened
     1 cup packed brown sugar
     1/2 cup brewed espresso
     1 egg
1-1/2 cups self-rising flour
     1/2 teaspoon ground cinnamon
     3/4 cup chopped slivered almonds, toasted
GLAZE:
1-1/2 cups confectioners' sugar
     3 tablespoons water
     3/4 teaspoon almond extract
     1/4 cup slivered almonds, toasted

**1.** In a large bowl, cream butter, brown sugar and espresso until blended. Beat in egg. Combine flour and cinnamon; gradually add to creamed mixture and mix well. Stir in chopped nuts. Spread into a greased 15-in. x 10-in. baking pan. Bake at 350° for 18-22 minutes or until lightly browned.

**2.** In a small bowl, combine confectioners' sugar, water and extract until smooth; spread over warm bars. Sprinkle with nuts. Cool on a wire rack. Cut into bars. **Yield:** 4 dozen.

**Editor's Note:** As a substitute for 1-1/2 cups self-rising flour, place 2-1/4 teaspoons baking powder and 3/4 teaspoon salt in a measuring cup. Add all-purpose flour to measure 1 cup. Combine with an additional 1/2 cup all-purpose flour.

## Pizzelle

*This recipe was adapted from one used by my Italian-born mother and grandmother. They used old irons on a gas stove, but now we have the convenience of electric pizzelle irons. The cookies are so delectable and beautiful, they're worth it!*
~Elizabeth Schwartz, Trevorton, Pennsylvania

*Pizzelle*

     18 eggs
3-1/2 cups sugar
1-1/4 cups canola oil
     1 tablespoon anise oil
6-1/2 cups all-purpose flour

**1.** In a large bowl, beat the eggs, sugar and oils until smooth. Gradually add flour and mix well.

**2.** Bake in a preheated pizzelle iron according to manufacturer's directions until golden brown. Remove to wire racks to cool. Store in an airtight container. **Yield:** 7 dozen.

## Pine Nut Cookies

*These simple goodies are rich and delicious—like little pats of butter! Pine nuts on top give these drop cookies a pleasant crunch.*
~Mercene Evans, Newport, Pennsylvania

     1 package (7 ounces) almond paste, grated
     1/2 cup sugar
     1/2 cup confectioners' sugar
     2 egg whites
     1/2 teaspoon vanilla extract
     3 tablespoons all-purpose flour
Pinch salt
     1/2 cup pine nuts

**1.** In a large bowl, beat the almond paste and sugars until crumbly. Beat in egg whites and vanilla. Combine flour and salt; gradually add to almond mixture and mix well. Cover and refrigerate for 1-2 hours or until easy to handle.

**2.** Place pine nuts in a shallow bowl. Working one at a time, with greased hands, drop dough by rounded teaspoonfuls into pine nuts. Place cookies nut side up 2 in. apart onto parchment paper-lined baking sheets.

**3.** Bake at 325° for 15-17 minutes or until edges begin to brown. Cool completely on baking sheets before carefully removing to wire racks. Store in an airtight container with waxed paper between layers. **Yield:** 2-1/2 dozen.

*Lemon Thins*

# Lemon Thins

*These irresistible thins have a tart lemon taste and crisp texture. For an extra-special dessert, put some of the cookies in bowls of chocolate ice cream.*        ~Judy Wilson, Sun City West, Arizona

   1/3 cup butter, softened
   1/3 cup shortening
     1 cup sugar
     2 tablespoons lemon juice
     2 teaspoons grated lemon peel
   1/2 teaspoon lemon extract
   1/2 teaspoon vanilla extract
1-1/2 cups all-purpose flour
1-1/2 teaspoons baking powder
   1/2 teaspoon baking soda
   1/4 teaspoon salt
     2 tablespoons confectioners' sugar

**1.** In a large bowl, cream the butter, shortening and sugar until light and fluffy. Beat in the lemon juice, lemon peel and extracts. Combine the flour, baking powder, baking soda and salt; gradually add to the creamed mixture. Shape into a 12-in. roll; wrap in plastic wrap. Refrigerate for at least 2 hours or until firm.

**2.** Unwrap dough; cut into 1/4-in. slices. Place 2 in. apart on ungreased baking sheets. Bake at 350° for 8-9 minutes or until the edges are lightly browned. Cool for 1-2 minutes before removing from pans to wire racks to cool completely. Dust with confectioners' sugar. **Yield:** 4-1/2 dozen.

# German Pecan Thins

*At Christmastime, it's fun to dig out those favorite holiday recipes your family loves. My kids would really miss these drizzled, candy-topped cookies if they weren't part of my treat selection.*
~Donna Lee Norvell, Jacksonville, Oregon

     1 cup butter, softened
     1 cup sugar

     1 cup packed brown sugar
     2 eggs
     1 teaspoon vanilla extract
     2 cups all-purpose flour
     1 teaspoon baking powder
     1 teaspoon baking soda
     1 teaspoon salt
     1 cup chopped pecans
     1 cup crushed cornflakes
**ICING:**
   1/3 cup water
   1/4 cup light corn syrup
     5 cups confectioners' sugar
   1/2 teaspoon vanilla extract
     1 cup red and green milk chocolate M&M's

**1.** In a large bowl, cream the butter and sugars until light and fluffy. Add eggs, one at a time, beating well after each addition. Beat in vanilla. Combine the flour, baking powder, baking soda and salt; gradually add to the creamed mixture. Stir in pecans and cornflakes.

**2.** Drop by tablespoonfuls 2 in. apart onto ungreased baking sheets. (Dough will spread during baking and cookies will be thin.) Bake at 350° for 10-12 minutes or until lightly browned. Cool for 2 minutes before removing from pans to wire racks.

**3.** In a large saucepan, combine water and corn syrup; bring to a boil. Remove from the heat. Gradually add confectioners' sugar and vanilla. Drizzle over cookies; top with M&M's. Store in an airtight container. **Yield:** 6 dozen.

# Hazelnut Crinkle Cookies

*I enjoy trying new recipes and always have willing "taste testers" at my house. Everyone gave these sugar-dusted goodies an enthusiastic thumbs-up!*        ~Janel Andrews, North Jerome, Idaho

     1 jar (13 ounces) chocolate hazelnut spread
   1/4 cup shortening
1-1/3 cups sugar
     2 eggs
     1 teaspoon vanilla extract
     3 cups all-purpose flour
     2 teaspoons baking powder
   1/2 teaspoon salt
   1/3 cup milk
2-1/2 cups chopped hazelnuts, toasted, *divided*
   1/2 cup confectioners' sugar

**1.** In a large bowl, cream the hazelnut spread, shortening and sugar. Beat in eggs and vanilla. Combine the flour, baking powder and salt; add to creamed mixture alternately with the milk. Mix well. Fold in 1/2 cup hazelnuts. Cover and refrigerate for 30 minutes or until firm.

**2.** Finely chop the remaining hazelnuts. Place hazelnuts and confectioners' sugar in separate shallow bowls. Roll dough into 1-in. balls; roll in hazelnuts, then sugar. Place 1 in. apart on ungreased baking sheets. Bake at 375° for 10-12 minutes or until set and surface is cracked. Cool for 1 minute before removing from pans to wire racks. **Yield:** 7 dozen.

*Hazelnut Crinkle Cookies*

*Pumpkin Seed Toffee*
*Praline Pecans & Cranberries (p. 72)*
*Cashew Clusters*

# Enchanting Candy

**Indulge the sweet tooths among your family and friends with luscious chocolates, rich truffles and more—all dressed up for the holiday season!**

## Cashew Clusters

*Three kinds of chocolate and white candy coating combine to make a rich, velvety exterior for these chunky clusters. They disappear fast!* ~Betsy Grantier, Charlottesville, Virginia

　　1 pound white candy coating, coarsely chopped
　　1 cup (6 ounces) semisweet chocolate chips
　　1 package (4 ounces) German sweet chocolate, coarsely chopped
　1/3 cup milk chocolate chips
　　1 can (9-3/4 ounces) salted whole cashews
　　1 can (9-1/4 ounces) salted cashew halves and pieces

**1.** In a large microwave-safe bowl, combine the first four ingredients. Cover and microwave at 50% power until melted, stirring every 30 seconds.

**2.** Stir in nuts. Drop by tablespoonfuls onto waxed paper-lined pans. Let stand until set. Store in an airtight container. **Yield:** 6 dozen.

**Editor's Note:** This recipe was tested in a 1,100-watt microwave.

## Pumpkin Seed Toffee

*My children and I have a tradition of saving our pumpkin seeds from the fall to use in recipes throughout the year. This spiced toffee is one of our best creations.* ~Suzanne Earl, Vernal, Utah

　　2 teaspoons plus 2 cups butter, softened, *divided*
　　2 cups sugar
　　1 tablespoon corn syrup
　　1 teaspoon pumpkin pie spice
　1/4 teaspoon salt
　　1 cup roasted pumpkin seeds *or* pepitas

**1.** Grease a 15-in. x 10-in. pan with 2 teaspoons butter; set aside. In a heavy saucepan, melt remaining butter. Stir in sugar, corn syrup, spice and salt. Cook and stir over medium heat until a candy thermometer reads 300° (hard-crack stage).

**2.** Remove from the heat; stir in pumpkin seeds. Immediately pour into prepared pan. Let stand at room temperature until cool, about 1 hour. Break into bite-size pieces. Store in an airtight container at room temperature. **Yield:** 2 pounds.

## Angel Food Candy

*I make lots of this "fairy food" to give as gifts each Christmas. To mix things up, I coat some of the candy in milk chocolate and some in dark.* ~Geralyn Emmerich, Hubertus, Wisconsin

　　1 teaspoon butter
　　1 cup sugar
　　1 cup dark corn syrup
　　1 tablespoon white vinegar
　　1 tablespoon baking soda
　1/2 pound dark chocolate candy coating, chopped
　　1 teaspoon shortening, *divided*
　1/2 pound milk chocolate candy coating, chopped

**1.** Line a 9-in. square pan with foil and grease the foil with butter; set aside. In a large heavy saucepan, combine the sugar, corn syrup and vinegar. Cook and stir over medium heat until sugar is dissolved. Bring to a boil. Cook, without stirring, until a candy thermometer reads 300° (hard-crack stage).

**2.** Remove from the heat; stir in baking soda. Immediately pour into prepared pan. Do not spread candy. Cool, then using foil, lift candy out of pan. Gently peel off foil; break candy into pieces.

**3.** In a microwave, melt dark chocolate coating and 1/2 teaspoon shortening; stir until smooth. Dip half the candies in the melted dark chocolate mixture, allowing excess to drip off. Place on waxed paper; let stand until set. Repeat with milk chocolate coating and remaining shortening and candies. Store in an airtight container. **Yield:** about 1-1/4 pounds.

**Editor's Note:** We recommend that you test your candy thermometer before each use by bringing water to a boil; the thermometer should read 212°. Adjust your recipe temperature up or down based on your test.

*Angel Food Candy*

## Sugared Walnuts

*If you're looking for a hunger-busting snack to tide over guests, give these sweet and crunchy walnuts a try. Toasted brown with a light sugar coating, they're guaranteed to please.*
*~Brenda Osborne, Cleveland, Tennessee*

3 cups walnut halves
1 cup sugar
1/2 cup strong brewed coffee
1 to 1-1/2 teaspoons ground cinnamon
1/2 teaspoon salt
1 teaspoon vanilla extract

**1.** Spread the walnut halves in a single layer on a baking sheet. Bake at 350° for 5 minutes or until heated through. Cover and keep warm.

**2.** In a large heavy saucepan, combine the sugar, coffee, cinnamon and salt. Bring to a boil over medium heat. Cook, without stirring, until a candy thermometer reads 250° (hard-ball stage). Remove from the heat; stir in vanilla. Add warm walnuts; toss to coat.

**3.** Pour walnuts into a greased 15-in. x 10-in. pan; separate with a fork. Cool. Store in an airtight container in the refrigerator. **Yield:** 4 cups.

## So-Easy Truffles

*These rich, three-ingredient treats with a creamy filling truly are as fuss-free to make as the name implies. Plus, the recipe includes two simple variations—Peanut Butter Truffles and Vanilla Cookie Truffles.*
*~Denise Kutchko, Odessa, Missouri*

1 package (18 ounces) cream-filled chocolate
   sandwich cookies
1 package (8 ounces) cream cheese, cubed
1 cup chocolate wafer crumbs

*So-Easy Truffles*

Place the chocolate sandwich cookies in a food processor; cover and process until finely crushed. Add the cream cheese; process until blended. Roll into 1-in. balls. Roll in wafer crumbs. Store in an airtight container in the refrigerator. **Yield:** 4 dozen.

**Peanut Butter Truffles:** Substitute a 16-oz. package of peanut butter cream-filled sandwich cookies for the chocolate sandwich cookies. Omit chocolate wafer crumbs. Melt 12 ounces of milk chocolate candy coating; stir until smooth. Dip balls in chocolate; place on waxed paper until set. Store in the refrigerator. **Yield:** 4 dozen.

**Vanilla Cookie Truffles:** Substitute a 16-oz. package of cream-filled vanilla sandwich cookies for the chocolate sandwich cookies. Melt 12 ounces of milk chocolate candy coating; stir until smooth. Dip balls in chocolate; sprinkle with 1/4 cup chocolate crumbs. Place on waxed paper until set. Store in the refrigerator. **Yield:** 4 dozen.

## Praline Pecans & Cranberries

(Pictured on page 70)

*When I came across the recipe for this pecan-cranberry candy, I decided to serve it as part of my Christmas spread. It was a big hit!* *~Nancy Roman, Hackensack, New Jersey*

3-1/2 cups pecan halves
1/4 cup packed brown sugar
1/4 cup light corn syrup
2 tablespoons butter
1 teaspoon vanilla extract
1/4 teaspoon baking soda
1-1/2 cups dried cranberries

**1.** Place pecans in a greased 13-in. x 9-in. baking pan; set aside. In a small saucepan, combine the brown sugar, corn syrup and butter. Bring to a boil over medium heat, stirring constantly. Remove from the heat. Stir in vanilla and baking soda. Drizzle over pecans; stir until coated.

**2.** Bake at 250° for 1 hour, stirring every 20 minutes. Add cranberries; toss to combine. Immediately transfer to a waxed paper-lined baking sheet; cool completely. Break into pieces. Store in an airtight container. **Yield:** 5-1/2 cups.

**Editor's Note:** We recommend that you test your candy thermometer before each use by bringing water to a boil; the thermometer should read 212°. Adjust your recipe temperature up or down based on your test.

## Walnut Peanut Butter Fudge

*Even if you already have a favorite recipe for fudge, you'll want to try this smooth, two-layer version. It simply melts in your mouth! Everyone likes the robust peanut butter taste and the nice crunch that comes from a sprinkling of walnuts on top.*
*~Robin Hazzard, Howes Cave, New York*

11 tablespoons butter, softened, *divided*
2 cups sugar

1 cup evaporated milk
1 teaspoon salt
1 package (10 ounces) peanut butter chips
1/2 cup packed brown sugar
1/2 cup light corn syrup
2 cups confectioners' sugar
1 cup chopped walnuts

**1.** Line a 9-in. square pan with foil and grease the foil with 1 tablespoon butter; set aside. In a heavy saucepan, combine sugar, evaporated milk, salt and 4 tablespoons butter. Cook and stir over medium heat until mixture comes to a rapid boil. Boil for 8 minutes or until a candy thermometer reads 226°, stirring constantly. Remove from the heat. Add peanut butter chips; stir until mixture is smooth. Pour into prepared pan. Refrigerate for 30 minutes.

**2.** Meanwhile, in a heavy saucepan, combine brown sugar, corn syrup and remaining butter. Cook and stir until smooth. Bring to a boil over medium heat. Remove from the heat. Stir in confectioners' sugar until smooth.

**3.** Spread evenly over peanut butter layer in pan. Sprinkle with walnuts; press down lightly. Refrigerate for 2 hours or until firm. Using foil, lift fudge out of pan. Cut into 1-in. squares. Store in an airtight container in the refrigerator. **Yield:** 3-1/4 pounds.

**Editor's Note:** We recommend that you test your candy thermometer before each use by bringing water to a boil; the thermometer should read 212°. Adjust your recipe temperature up or down based on your test.

# Peppermint Taffy

*Here's an old-fashioned delight—chewy candy with a mild peppermint flavor and just the right amount of sweetness. It's a snap to make and isn't as stiff as the taffy found in stores.*
*~Suzette Jury, Keene, California*

1 tablespoon plus 1/4 cup butter, cubed
2 cups light corn syrup
1-1/2 cups sugar
2 teaspoons peppermint extract
1/2 teaspoon salt
6 drops red food coloring, optional

**1.** Grease a 15-in. x 10-in. pan with 1 tablespoon butter; set aside. In a heavy small saucepan, combine corn syrup and sugar. Bring to a boil over medium heat. Add remaining butter; stir until melted. Cook and stir until a candy thermometer reads 250° (hard-ball stage).

**2.** Remove from the heat; stir in peppermint extract, salt and food coloring if desired (keep your face away from mixture as the odor is very strong). Pour into prepared pan. Let stand for 5-10 minutes or until cool enough to handle. Divide into 4 portions.

**3.** With well-buttered fingers, quickly pull one portion of the candy until firm but pliable (the color will become light pink). Pull into a 1/2-in.-wide rope. Repeat with the remain-

*Peppermint Taffy*

ing candy. Cut into 1-in. pieces. Wrap each piece in waxed paper. **Yield:** 1-3/4 pounds.

**Editor's Note:** We recommend that you test your candy thermometer before each use by bringing water to a boil; the thermometer should read 212°. Adjust your recipe temperature up or down based on your test.

# Cranberry Butter Crunch Bark

*This treat is like a combination of almond bark and buttercrunch toffee, with festive red color from cranberries. It's decadent and addictive!* *~Heather Ferris, Vanderhoof, British Columbia*

1-1/2 teaspoons plus 1 cup butter, *divided*
1 cup sugar
3 tablespoons water
8 cups chopped white candy coating (about 3 pounds), *divided*
3 cups dried cranberries, *divided*

**1.** Grease a 15-in. x 10-in. pan with 1/2 teaspoon butter. In a heavy saucepan over medium-low heat, bring 1 cup butter, sugar and water to a boil, stirring constantly. Cook over medium heat until a candy thermometer reads 290° (soft-crack stage). Pour into prepared pan (do not scrape sides of saucepan). Refrigerate for 1 hour or until hard.

**2.** Break toffee into pieces. Place in a food processor; cover and process until coarsely chopped. Divide in half; set aside. Butter two 15-in. x 10-in. pans with remaining butter. In a microwave, melt 4 cups white candy coating. Stir in 1-1/2 cups dried cranberries and half of reserved toffee pieces.

**3.** Pour into one prepared pan; spread to edges of pan. Repeat with remaining white candy coating, dried cranberries and toffee pieces. **Yield:** 4 pounds.

**Editor's Note:** We recommend that you test your candy thermometer before each use by bringing water to a boil; the thermometer should read 212°. Adjust your recipe temperature up or down based on your test.

## A Crafted Snowman

*Ferne Nicolaisen, Cherokee, Iowa*

I think I'll make a snowman
On this chilly winter's day.
I'll build him in my crafting room
To chase the blues away.

Should I make him tall and lean?
Or maybe short and fat?
Should he be a gentleman
And wear a stovepipe hat?

Should he wear a scarf of red?
Have buttons big and bold?
Should he be so very young?
Or maybe very old?

Does he need some earmuffs
And perhaps some feet to stand?
Yes, he'll wear a happy smile
And gloves upon his hands.

Gazing out the window
With my thoughts of years now past,
I'll build this crafty snowman
So he'll last and last and last.

# Forget It, Santa

Ida Pardue, Big Bear Lake, California

She opened the teddy bear,
Dolly, bright blocks
And the picture book playing
Sweet nursery tunes.

Then all day on Christmas
She played, not with those,
But instead with my same
kitchen measuring spoons!

# Build Your Own
# Santa's Workshop!

CHRISTMAS EVE is just around the corner…and the elves in Santa's workshop are as busy as can be, making dolls, games and toys for good girls and boys.

It's a magical scene that fills the imagination of every child during the holiday season. This year, why not re-create that merry image for your family and friends? It's fun with the sweet idea here!

The fanciful Santa's Workshop Cupcakes, created by our Test Kitchen home economists, are sure to charm both young and old alike. And you can easily assemble these yummy goodies yourself following the simple, step-by-step directions in the recipe below.

Your holiday guests will be amazed and enchanted by all of the adorable details—from Santa and his list to the toy drums, pull car, gift boxes and train. Each cake and candy confection is child's play to create and a treat to eat.

So why not make like an elf? Build your own North Pole delight…and work some Christmastime magic!

## Santa's Workshop Cupcakes

Cupcakes and miniature cupcakes of your choice
1 to 2 cans vanilla frosting (16 ounces *each*)
New paintbrush, pencil, paper and waxed paper
**BEACH BALLS:**
 Fruit Roll-Ups
 Sour fruit hard candy balls
**BLOCKS:**
 Alphabet cinnamon-graham cookies
 Assorted food coloring
**CAR PULL-TOY:**
 Life Savers Gummies and circus peanut candy
 Candy-coated sunflower kernels
 Red shoestring licorice
**DOG:**
 Tootsie Roll Small Midgees
 Fruit Roll-Up
 Dragee
**DRUM:**
 Fruit Roll-Up
 Dragees
**PRESENTS:**
 Fruit Roll-Ups
 Starburst candies
**TEDDY BEAR:**
 Tootsie Roll Small Midgees
 Fruit Roll-Up
**TRAIN:**
 Individual cream-filled sponge cake
 Sprinkles of your choice
 Candy-coated milk chocolate miniature kiss and black
  licorice coin
 Vanilla wafer and miniature peanut butter-filled
  sandwich crackers
 Dragees
**SANTA AND ELVES:**
 White and chocolate candy coating
 Ivory and blue paste food coloring
 Red and green sprinkles

Red shoestring licorice
Candy-coated sunflower kernels
Starburst candies
Miniature marshmallows
Corn syrup
White nonpareils
Dots candies and milk chocolate M&M's
**LIST:**
 Ready-to-use white rolled fondant
 Food writing pen

**For beach balls:** Referring to Fig. 1 on page 79, cut oval shapes with pointed ends from Fruit Roll-Ups. Position on each hard candy ball; press to attach.

**For blocks:** Attach four graham cookies with frosting to form the four sides of a box; attach another cookie to the top. Using a new paintbrush, brush food coloring over cookies to color as desired.

**For car pull-toy:** Using frosting, attach Life Savers Gummies to circus peanut, forming tires. Insert a sunflower kernel into center of each tire. For pull-rope, loop a 4-in. piece of shoestring licorice; insert into peanut.

**For dog:** Place two Tootsie Rolls on a small piece of waxed paper; microwave on high for 5-7 seconds or until softened. Referring to Fig. 2, break off desired amount for body; roll into a rounded triangle shape. Roll two smaller pieces into legs; press onto front of body to attach. Roll another piece into an oval shape for head; attach two small pieces for ears. Press head onto body; attach a small piece for tail.

Referring to Fig. 3, wrap a thin strip of Fruit Roll-Up around dog's neck for collar. Form another strip of Fruit Roll-Up into a bow; press onto collar to attach. Attach a dragee to center of bow with frosting. Pipe a small amount of frosting to make eyes.

**For drum:** Remove a miniature cupcake from paper liner. Place cupcake upside-down. Spread frosting over the top and sides. Decorate drum with thin strips of Fruit Roll-Ups. Using frosting, attach dragees as desired.

**For presents:** Cut a Fruit Roll-Up into thin strips. Place two strips widthwise around desired number of stacked Starburst candies; press together at base to attach. For bow, form two Fruit Roll-Up strips into figure eights; press together in center and press on top of wrapped candy.

**For teddy bear:** Place a Tootsie Roll on a small piece of waxed paper; microwave on high for 5-7 seconds or until softened. Referring to Fig. 2, break off desired amount for body; roll into a rounded oval shape. Roll two smaller pieces into arms and two pieces into legs. Press onto body to attach. Roll another piece into a ball for head; attach two small pieces for ears and one for nose. Press head onto body.

Referring to Fig. 3, wrap a thin strip of Fruit Roll-Up around bear's neck. Form another strip of Fruit Roll-Up into a bow; press onto ribbon to attach. Pipe a small amount of frosting to make eyes.

**For train:** Cut a thin slice from one end of sponge cake to allow it to stand vertically. Frost top and sides of sponge

*(Continued on next page)*

cake; coat with sprinkles. Stand on serving platter. Frost one cupcake; dip the top in sprinkles. Place cupcake so the bottom is against the flat side of sponge cake.

For smokestack, attach a miniature kiss to top of cupcake with frosting. Attach licorice coin to center front of cupcake. Attach a vanilla wafer to sponge cake for large wheel.

For train cars, frost desired number of miniature cupcakes; dip the tops in sprinkles. Arrange cupcakes on their sides behind train engine. Place a sandwich cracker at the base of each car. Pipe window and wheel details with frosting; decorate with dragees as desired.

**For Santa and elves:** With a pencil and paper, draw a beard, a mustache, eyes, eyebrows, ears and hair pieces. Melt white and chocolate candy coatings in separate microwave-safe bowls; stir until smooth.

Divide white coating into three portions; tint one portion ivory and another blue. Transfer each to a resealable plastic bag; cut a small hole in the corner of each bag. Referring to Fig. 4, place waxed paper over the drawings. Working quickly, pipe coating over designs. Using chocolate coating, pipe a small dot into the center of each eye. Refrigerate until set.

Frost a cupcake; dip the top in red sprinkles for Santa's body. For each elf, frost a miniature cupcake; dip the top in green sprinkles.

Tint a small amount of frosting ivory. Using ivory frosting, frost one cupcake for Santa's head and one miniature cupcake

for each elf's head. Lay an ivory cupcake on its side on top of each sprinkled cupcake; secure each with a toothpick.

Gently lift candy features from waxed paper; arrange on cupcakes. Form smiles with shoestring licorice; use sunflower kernels for noses.

For Santa hat, place four red Starburst candies on a piece of waxed paper; microwave on high for 3-5 seconds or until softened. Referring to Fig. 5, place candies side by side; using a rolling pin, roll candies together to 1/8-in. thickness. Cut into a triangle; form into a cone shape. Press seam to seal; gently form into a hat shape around a small ball of plastic wrap. Repeat for elf hats using three candies for each hat.

For pom-poms, cut marshmallows in half; roll each half in corn syrup, then in nonpareils. Press onto the tip of hats and around brims. Attach Dots candies, M&M's or additional pom-poms to elves to form collars. Remove plastic wrap from inside hats; attach to heads with frosting.

**For list:** Roll out fondant; cut to form a long narrow strip for list. Write names with food writing pen. Keep covered until ready to use.

**Finishing touches:** Arrange cupcakes on tiered serving platters. Add balls, blocks, cars, dogs, presents, teddy bears and additional assorted candies as desired; gently drape list down tiers. **Yield:** varies.

**Editor's Note:** This recipe was tested with Newman's Own alphabet cinnamon-graham cookies for the blocks.

## *Serving Santa's Workshop*

THE CUPCAKES and candy confections in the Santa's Workshop Cupcakes display are just as fun to eat as they are to make. Before serving, keep in mind the following helpful hints:

▲ The cupcakes (Santa, elves, toy train and drums) are best served the day they are assembled. Using ready-made cupcakes from the grocery store or bakery will help speed up assembly.

▲ The toy car, dog, teddy bear, presents, blocks and balls may be assembled up to a week before serving and stored in an airtight container.

▲ Santa's fondant list of names may also be assembled in advance if it is shaped in the desired "draped" position before it hardens.

▲ Remember to remove the toothpicks from the Santa and elf cupcakes before serving.

# Santa's Workshop How-tos

*Refer to these helpful how-to photos while assembling the Santa's Workshop Cupcakes (p. 77). You'll have merry Christmas treats in no time!*

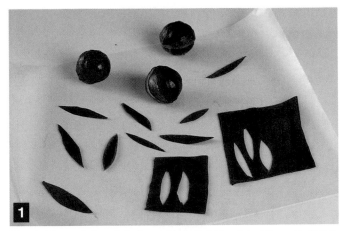

**Fig. 1:** For each beach ball, cut Fruit Roll-Ups into thin oval shapes with pointed ends to resemble the sections of a beach ball. Press the shapes side-by-side, alternating the colors, onto a hard candy ball.

**Fig. 2:** Shape softened Tootsie Rolls into body parts and press them together to create the dog and teddy bear. Cut Fruit Roll-Ups into strips to create the dog's collar and the bow around the bear's neck.

**Fig. 3:** Press a Fruit Roll-Up strip around the neck of the dog and teddy bear. Press a bow onto each and add a dragee to the dog. Pipe a small amount of white frosting to create eyes.

**Fig. 4:** For the Santa and elf cupcakes, draw the facial features onto paper and place waxed paper over it. Using candy coating, pipe the facial features onto the waxed paper following the drawings beneath.

**Fig. 5:** For each hat, roll out softened Starburst candies to a 1/8-inch thickness and cut out a triangle. Form the triangle into a cone and gently shape the cone into a hat around a small ball of plastic wrap.

# Seasonal Crafts

The most heartwarming decorations and gifts are handmade ones. With the simple projects in this chapter, you can easily make your own holiday creations to brighten the Christmas season.

# Joyful Pillow Will Accent Your Decor

*SPREAD CHEER to just about any room with this December decor from Sue Childress of Judson, Texas. Her filet crochet design transformed a plain red pillow into a merry showpiece.*

## MATERIALS:
Chart on this page
One 200-yard ball of size 5 white crochet cotton (Sue used Grignasco Cotton 5)
Size B (2.25mm) crochet hook (or size needed to obtain correct gauge)
12-inch x 16-inch pillow form or polyester stuffing
Two 13-inch x 17-inch pieces of red fabric for pillow
All-purpose thread—red and white
2 yards of 1/2-inch-wide beaded trim
Standard sewing supplies

**GAUGE:** When working with a size B hook, 9 dcs and 3 rows = 1 inch.

**READING CHART:** Each row between Row 1 and the last row begins and ends with 3 dcs.

All the vertical lines on the chart = 1 dc.
The ■ on the chart = 1 dc.
The "X" on the chart = dc2tog.
The horizontal line on the chart = ch 1.

## SPECIAL STITCH:
**Dc2tog:** Yo, insert hk in next st, yo drawing up a lp, yo and draw thread through 2 lps on hk, yo, insert hk in same ch-sp, yo drawing up a lp, yo and draw thread through 2 lps, yo and draw thread through remaining three loops on hk.

**FINISHED SIZE:** Pillow is 16 inches wide x 12 inches high.

## DIRECTIONS:
**Row 1:** Ch 66, dc in fourth ch from hk, dc in each remaining ch across, turn: 64 dcs.

**Row 2:** Ch 3 for first dc, work 2 dcs in next dc, ch 1, [sk next dc, dc in next dc, ch 1] across to last 2 sts, work 2 dcs in next st, dc in last st (turning ch), turn: 3 dcs, 30 sps, 3 dcs.

**Row 3:** Ch 3 for first dc, work 2 dcs in next dc, ch 1, [dc in next dc, ch 1] across to last 2 sts, work 2 dcs in next st, dc in last st (turning ch), turn: 3 dcs, 30 sps, 3 dcs.

**Rows 4-42:** Follow chart, beginning each row with ch 3, 2 dcs and ending each row with 3 dcs.

**Row 43:** Dc in each dc and ch-sp across: 64 dcs.

**EDGING: Round 1:** Working around the post of sts at end of row, * work 2 scs in first row, [sk next row, work 9 trs in next row, sk next row, work 2 scs in next row] across to end. Across end, [sk 2 dcs, work 9 trs in next dc, sk 2 dcs, sc in next 2 dcs] across; repeat from * to beginning sc.

**Round 2:** [Ch 4, sk next st, sc in next st] around, join with a sl st in first ch of beginning ch-4. Fasten off.

Weave in all loose ends.

**PILLOW:** With right sides together and edges matching, sew the two pieces of red fabric together with red thread and a 1/2-inch seam, leaving an opening for turning and stuffing. Clip corners diagonally.

Turn pillow right side out and insert pillow form or stuffing. Turn raw edges of opening in and hand-sew closed.

**FINISHING:** Wet-block crocheted piece. Let dry.

With white thread, hand-tack crocheted piece to front of pillow. With white thread, hand-tack beaded trim to inside edge of edging as shown in photo at far left, overlapping ends and trimming excess. ❀

### STITCH KEY
■ = 1 dc
☐ Ch 1, sk 1 ch
Ⓧ Dc2tog
Space over X = ch 1, sk dc2tog
X over space = dc2tog in ch space
X over x = dc2tog

**FILET CROCHET CHART**

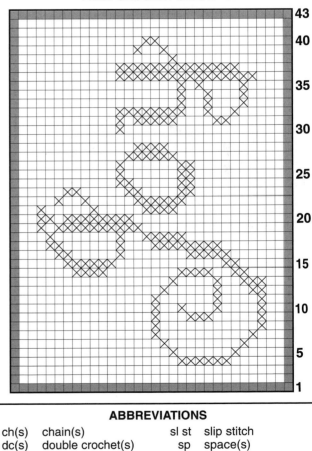

### ABBREVIATIONS

| | | | |
|---|---|---|---|
| ch(s) | chain(s) | sl st | slip stitch |
| dc(s) | double crochet(s) | sp | space(s) |
| hk | hook | st(s) | stitch(es) |
| sc(s) | single crochet(s) | tr(s) | treble crochet(s) |
| sk | skip | yo | yarn over |

* [ ] Instructions following asterisk or between brackets are repeated as directed.

## Folksy Pine Will Punch Up Your Home

*BRANCH OUT from the usual needlework with this traditional trim. "Needle punch is a simple technique," assures Brenda Tapia from Federal Way, Washington. "This little tree can be finished in about an evening."*

**MATERIALS NEEDED:**
Pattern on this page
8-inch square of weaver's cloth
Quilter's marking pen or pencil
6-inch embroidery hoop
Needle punch tool with medium needle and threader
  (see Editor's Note)
DMC six-strand embroidery floss in colors listed on
  color key
Embroidery needle
Fabric glue
3-1/2-inch x 4-1/2-inch unfinished wooden frame
Water container
Foam plate or palette
Paper towels
Acrylic paint—black and barn red
Small flat paintbrush
Sandpaper
Varnish
Scissors

**EDITOR'S NOTE:** Punch needle embroidery is worked through tightly woven fabric that is placed in an embroidery hoop. Loops of floss or thread are formed on the opposite side of the working surface to create the design.

A special tool with a hollow needle is needed to feed the floss or thread as the needle is punched through. Punch needle supplies are sold at most craft stores.

**FINISHED SIZE:** Framed tree measures 4-1/2 inches high x 3-1/2 inches wide.

**DIRECTIONS:**
**GENERAL PUNCH NEEDLE DIRECTIONS:** Use 30- to 40-inch-long lengths of floss.

If your punch needle tool has adjustable settings, set it so the needle tip is about 1/2 inch long.

Hold the tool perpendicular to the fabric. Work with the slanted edge of the tool facing the front or to the side, but never to the back.

The floss that is coming out of the top of the hollow tube should be behind your hand. There should be no tension on the feeder floss.

Push (punch) the needle all the way through the fabric. Lift the needle out until the tip appears, then slide the tip a short distance and punch again. Check to see if the loops formed are the desired length. If needed, adjust the length of the needle.

As you work, loops will appear on the underside of the fabric and a short running stitch will appear on the upper side.

Trim the tail of thread from the starting point after you have worked a few stitches, leaving about 1/8 inch of floss. Do not pull on the tail or you will remove your stitches.

When the end of the feeder floss reaches the top of the hollow tube, work a few more stitches. Then hold the last stitch in place with your finger. Lift the needle from the fabric and trim the tail of floss as before.

Add a drop of fabric glue to the ends of floss to secure them in place.

Check the front of your work periodically to make sure your loops are the same height and are evenly spaced.

**PREPARATION:** Center square of weaver's cloth wrong side up over tree pattern.

Use quilter's marking pen or pencil to transfer pattern onto cloth.

With design centered, place marked cloth right side up in embroidery hoop, making sure cloth is tight and secure.

**PUNCH NEEDLE TREE:** Follow instructions that come with the punch needle tool to thread tool. Use unseparated floss (six strands) for all needle punching.

Thread tool with Topaz floss and fill in star with stitches

**TREE PATTERN**
Trace 1—weaver's cloth

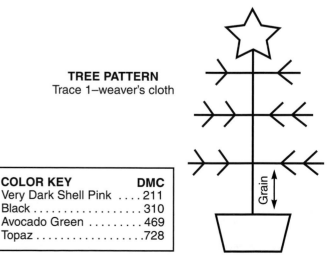

| COLOR KEY | DMC |
|---|---|
| Very Dark Shell Pink | 211 |
| Black | 310 |
| Avocado Green | 469 |
| Topaz | 728 |

worked very close together.

Thread tool with Avocado Green floss and fill in the tree trunk and branches.

Thread tool with Very Dark Shell Pink floss and fill in the tree stand.

Thread tool with Black floss and fill in the background.

FRAME: Remove back of frame.

Place small amounts of paint on palette or foam plate as needed while painting the frame as directed in the instructions that follow.

Paint frame black. Let dry.

Paint frame barn red. Let dry.

When completely dry, sand frame to reveal some of the black color underneath as shown in the photo at far left.

Wipe the frame with a damp paper towel to remove sanding dust.

Apply varnish to frame following manufacturer's instructions. Let dry.

FINISHING: Center finished tree design right side up over cardboard piece from frame. Trim excess weaver's cloth, leaving about 1 inch on all sides.

Wrap edges of weaver's cloth to back of cardboard piece.

Stitch across back of cardboard piece from side to side and top to bottom to hold edges in place.

Insert completed tree design into frame and replace back of frame. ❀

---

# Ring in Christmas With Painted Bell

*JINGLE all the way through winter with this snowman accent from Irene Wegener of Corning, New York. She transformed a small rusty bell using simple painting and a ribbon hanger.*

MATERIALS NEEDED:
2-1/2-inch rusty liberty bell
Gloss spray sealer
Water basin
Paper towels
Foam plate or palette
Acrylic craft paints—black, brown, burnt orange, off-white, red and white
Paintbrushes—small flat, small angle brush and liner
Toothpick
Pencil
Ruler
Desired length of 1-inch-wide ribbon for hanger

FINISHED SIZE: Excluding hanger, bell measures about 2-1/2 inches across x 3 inches high.

DIRECTIONS:
Spray outside of liberty bell with gloss sealer following manufacturer's instructions. Let dry.

Keep paper towels and a container of water handy to clean paintbrushes. Place small amounts of paint as needed onto foam plate or palette. Add coats of paint as needed for complete coverage. Let paint dry after every application.

Refer to photo at right as a guide while painting as directed in the instructions that follow.

Use flat brush and off-white to paint a 1-inch circle on opposite sides of the bell for snowman's head.

Use angle brush and brown to shade around the outside edge of each head.

Dip toothpick into black and add seven tiny dots for mouth and two small dots for eyes.

Use liner and black to add eyebrows.

Use angle brush and orange to paint nose.

Dip toothpick into white and add a tiny dot to each eye.

Dip angle brush into red and wipe off excess paint onto paper towel. With a nearly dry brush and a circular motion, add cheeks to each head.

Use liner and white to write "SNOWBELLS RING… ARE YOU LISTENING?" around bottom rim of bell. Dip toothpick into white and add a dot to ends of letters.

Use liner and white to add random snowflakes around the bell. For each snowflake, make an "X" and then add another line through the X. Dip toothpick into white and add a dot to the end of each line.

When paint is dry, add another coat of spray sealer.

Thread the ribbon through the top of the bell. Tie the ends in a bow for hanger. ❀

# Have a Ball with Ping Pong Snowmen

*YOU'LL have a hit when you make these sporty ornaments. "One day while shopping, I saw ping pong balls," says Susan Newberry of DeFuniak Springs, Florida. "And I dreamed up these!"*

**MATERIALS NEEDED** (for all):
Three ping-pong balls
Ice pick or awl
Toothpick
Scrap of Styrofoam to use as holder for painting
Paper towels
Water container
Foam plate or palette
Acrylic craft paints—red and white
Orange dimensional paint
Paintbrushes—small flat and liner
Glue gun and glue sticks
Three 12-inch lengths of gold cord for hanging loops
Hand-sewing needle
Standard sewing supplies
(For snowman with red hat cuff):
5-1/4-inch x 7-inch piece of red print Polarfleece fabric
    with stretchy edge along the short side for hat
2-inch x 5-1/4-inch piece of red solid Polarfleece with
    stretchy edge along the long side for cuff
Six doll buttons—three green and three yellow
(For snowman with yellow hat cuff):
Pattern on this page
Tracing paper and pencil
5-1/4-inch x 6-inch piece of red print Polarfleece fabric
    with stretchy edge along the short side for hat
2-inch x 5-1/4-inch piece of yellow solid Polarfleece with
    stretchy edge along the long side for cuff
Pom-poms—four 1/4-inch green, three 1/4-inch red and
    one 3/4-inch green
(For earmuff snowman):
Two 3/4-inch orange pom-poms

3-inch length of black chenille stem
1-inch x 8-inch piece of blue-and-orange print
    Polarfleece fabric for scarf

**FINISHED SIZE:** Excluding hanging loop, each ornament measures about 3 inches high x 3 inches wide.

**DIRECTIONS:**
**SNOWMAN HEAD (make three):** Use ice pick or awl to make a hole in a ping-pong ball. Insert one end of toothpick into hole. Push opposite end of toothpick into scrap of Styrofoam to hold the ball during painting.

Keep paper towels and a container of water handy to clean paintbrushes. Place small amount of paint as needed onto foam plate or palette. Add coats of paint as needed for complete coverage. Let paint dry after every application. Refer to photo at left as a guide while painting as directed in the instructions that follow.

Use flat brush and white to paint entire ping-pong ball.

With hole in ball at the top, add eyes, eyebrows and mouth to ball using black marker.

Use white and liner to add a small highlight to each eye.

Dip flat brush into red and wipe off excess paint onto paper towel. With a nearly dry brush and a circular motion, add cheeks.

Use liner and orange to add carrot nose. Let dry.
**SNOWMAN WITH RED HAT CUFF:** Pin the red solid fleece piece along a 5-1/4-inch edge of the print fleece piece with right sides together and edges matching. Sew along the pinned edge with a narrow seam.

Make 1-inch-long cuts about 1/4 inch apart along opposite short edge of the print piece for fringe.

Fold the hat piece in half with right sides together and edges matching. Pin as needed. Sew from the cuff to the fringed end with a narrow seam. Turn hat right side out.

Sew around edge of fringe with a basting stitch. Pull thread to gather edge together. Fasten off.

Turn cuff inside hat, leaving about 1/2 inch of red solid

**SNOWMAN HAT PATTERN**
Trace 1—folded
tracing paper
Cut 1—red print
Polarfleece

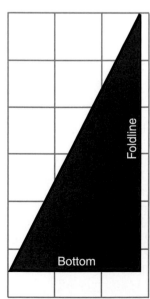

Foldline

Bottom

Each square = 1 inch

Use photocopier to enlarge
pattern 200% or draw a
1-inch grid on tracing paper
and draw pattern as shown
onto tracing paper

fabric showing. Glue as needed to hold. Let dry.

Finishing: Place hat on ball, covering hole in ball. Position hat with seam to the left side, making sure snowman's face shows. Glue as needed to hold. Let dry.

Glue buttons along cuff on front of hat. Let dry.

Hand-sew or glue fringe end of hat to side of cuff. Let dry.

Thread hand-sewing needle with cord. Stitch cord through top of hat. Tie ends of cord together for hanging loop.

SNOWMAN WITH YELLOW HAT CUFF: Trace enlarged hat pattern onto folded tracing paper with pencil. Cut out hat along traced outline and open for complete pattern.

Cut hat from red print fleece with the stretchy edge of fabric along the bottom edge of hat.

Pin the yellow solid fleece piece along the 5-1/4-inch edge of the red print fleece piece with right sides together and edges matching. Sew along the pinned edge with a narrow seam. Turn right side out.

Fold the hat piece in half with right sides together and edges matching. Pin as needed. Sew from the cuff to the point with a narrow seam. Turn hat right side out.

Turn cuff inside hat, leaving about 1/2 inch of the yellow solid fabric showing. Glue as needed to hold. Let dry.

Finishing: Place hat on ball, covering hole in ball. Position hat with seam to the left side, making sure snowman's face shows. Glue as needed to hold. Let dry.

Glue 1/4-inch pom-poms on front of hat cuff. Let dry.

Hand-sew or glue narrow end of hat to side of cuff. Let dry.

Glue 3/4-inch green pom-pom to tip of hat. Let dry.

Thread hand-sewing needle with cord. Stitch cord through top of hat. Tie ends of cord together for hanging loop.

EARMUFF SNOWMAN: Tie ends of cord together for hanging loop. Slip over chenille stem.

Glue chenille stem across the top of snowman's head, centering the hanging loop at the top. Let dry.

Glue an orange pom-pom to each side of snowman's head, covering ends of stem. Let dry.

Tie a loose overhand knot in center of scarf piece. Glue knotted area to bottom of snowman's head. Let dry. ❄

---

# Round Out Trees With Wreath Trim

*CIRCLE this idea if you need a super-seller for a holiday craft bazaar or fund-raiser. The lovely, lacy crocheted ornament from Peggy Moen of Foxboro, Wisconsin works up quickly.*

**MATERIALS NEEDED:**
Size 10 white crochet thread
Size 7 (1.5mm) steel crochet hook (or size needed to obtain correct gauge)
Scissors
Fabric stiffener
5-inch square of plastic-covered heavy cardboard
Rust-proof straight pins
Two 2-inch-long artificial holly leaves
Three small red artificial berries
18-inch length of 1/8-inch-wide red satin ribbon
Two 3-inch-long pearl sprays
Small flat paintbrush
Iridescent glitter
Glue gun and glue stick
8-inch length of monofilament thread for hanger

GAUGE: At the end of Round 2, center circle of wreath should measure about 1-1/4 inches across.

**SPECIAL STITCH:**
Dc cl = Double Crochet Cluster: Yo, insert hk in sp indicated, yo, draw yarn through the st, yo, draw yarn through two lps on hk, leaving the last lp of this dc on the hk, yo, insert hk in same sp, yo, draw yarn through the st, yo, draw through 2 lps on hk, leaving last lp of this dc on the hk (there are now 3 lps on hk), yo, pull yarn through all three lps on hk, ch 1 to close the cluster.

FINISHED SIZE: Wreath measures about 4 inches across.

DIRECTIONS:
CROCHETING: Round 1: Ch 30, join with a sl st in first ch made to form a ring.

Round 2: Ch 1 for first sc, sc in same st, sc in next ch, [work 2 scs in next ch, sc in each of next two chs] around, join with a sl st in ch-1: 40 scs.

Round 3: Ch 3 for first dc, dc in same sp, ch 1, to close the cl, [ch 3, sk 1 sc, work dc cl in next sc] around, ch 3, join

*(Continued on next page)*

with a sl st in top of first cl: 20 dc cls.

Round 4: Sl st into next ch-sp, ch 6, (counts as one dc and one ch-3), in same sp [dc, ch 3, dc, ch 3] four times, dc in same sp, sc in top of next dc cl, * [dc, ch 3] five times in next ch-3 sp, dc in same sp; repeat from * around, join with a sl st in third ch of beginning ch-6: 6 dcs in each ch-3 sp.

Round 5: Sl st in ch-3 sp, [ch 3, sl st in next ch-sp] four times, ch 3, sc in next sc, * [ch 3, sl st in next ch-sp] five times, ch 3, sc in next sc, repeat from * around. Fasten off. Weave in all loose ends.

STIFFENING: Apply stiffener to crocheted wreath following manufacturer's instructions.

Place crocheted wreath on plastic-covered cardboard and use pins to hold center of wreath in a circle. Use additional pins to hold outer chain spaces of wreath in place, forming a flat circle. Let dry.

FINISHING: Form ribbon into a multi-loop bow as shown in photo on page 85.

Referring to photo for position, glue holly leaves, pearl sprays, bow and berries to wreath. Let dry.

Use paintbrush to apply a small amount of stiffener to wreath, leaves and berries. While stiffener is still wet, sprinkle wreath with glitter. Let dry.

Insert end of monofilament thread through an opening at the top of wreath. Tie ends in a knot to form hanging loop. ❀

---

### ABBREVIATIONS

| | | | |
|---|---|---|---|
| ch(s) | chain(s) | sk | skip |
| cl(s) | cluster(s) | sl st | slip stitch |
| dc(s) | double crochet(s) | sp | space |
| hk | hook | st(s) | stitch(es) |
| lp(s) | loop(s) | yo | yarn over |
| sc(s) | single crochet(s) | | |

* [ ] Instructions following asterisk or
between brackets are repeated as directed.

---

# Stitched Bags Are Stuffed with Cheer

*JUST LIKE Santa's sack, these mini cross-stitched pouches can hold gifts—for example, jewelry or money. "Or hang them on the Christmas tree," says Ferne Nicolaisen of Cherokee, Iowa.*

MATERIALS NEEDED (for all):
Charts on next page
Off-white 14-count Aida cloth—three 3-1/4-inch x 5-inch pieces and three 7-inch squares
Matching all-purpose thread
DMC six-strand embroidery floss in colors listed on color key
Size 24 tapestry needle
Three 12-inch lengths of 1/8-inch-wide green satin ribbon
Large-eye hand-sewing needle
Polyester stuffing or small gift for each bag
Standard sewing supplies

FINISHED SIZE: Design area of Santa is 24 stitches high x 17 stitches wide and measures 2-1/4 inches high x 1-1/2 inches wide. Design area of poinsettia is 21 stitches high x 15 stitches wide and measures 1-7/8 inches high x 1-1/4 inches wide. Design area of ornament is 26 stitches high x 19 stitches wide and measures 2-5/8 inches high x 1-1/2 inches wide.

DIRECTIONS:
CROSS-STITCHING: Zigzag or overcast the edges of the 7-inch squares of Aida cloth to prevent fraying. To find the center, fold the 7-inch squares in half crosswise, then fold in half lengthwise and mark where the folds intersect.

Draw lines across the charts, connecting opposite arrows. Mark where lines intersect. Begin stitching here for a centered design.

Each square on charts represents one set of fabric threads surrounded by four holes. Each stitch is worked over one set of threads with the needle passing through the holes.

The color and/or symbol inside each square on the charts, along with the color key, indicates which color of six-strand embroidery floss to use to make the cross-stitches. The wide lines on the charts show where to make the backstitches. See Fig. 1 at right for stitch illustrations.

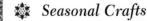

Use 18-inch lengths of floss. Longer strands tend to tangle and fray. Separate the strands of floss and thread the needle with two strands for all cross-stitches. Use one strand for backstitches and French knots.

To begin stitching, leave a 1-inch tail of floss on the back of the design and hold tail in place while working the first few stitches over it. To end stitching, run needle under a few stitches in back before clipping the floss close to work.

When all stitching is complete, and only if necessary, gently wash the stitched pieces in lukewarm water. Press right side down on a terry-cloth towel to dry.

**ASSEMBLY:** Trim the sides of each stitched piece to make a 3-1/4-inch-wide piece with the design centered. Then trim the top and bottom edges to make a 5-inch-high piece, positioning the top of each design about 2 inches from top edge.

Place each trimmed, stitched piece on top of an unstitched Aida cloth piece with right sides together and raw edges matching. Sew the side and bottom edges together with a narrow seam to make a pouch.

Turn each pouch right side out. Pull threads along raw edge to create fringe.

**FINISHING:** Place gift or stuffing inside each pouch.

Thread large-eye needle with a ribbon piece. Starting at center front of pouch about 1-1/4 inches from top edge, stitch around with a long running stitch, ending at center front. Remove needle and center ribbon. Tie ends in a bow. ❄

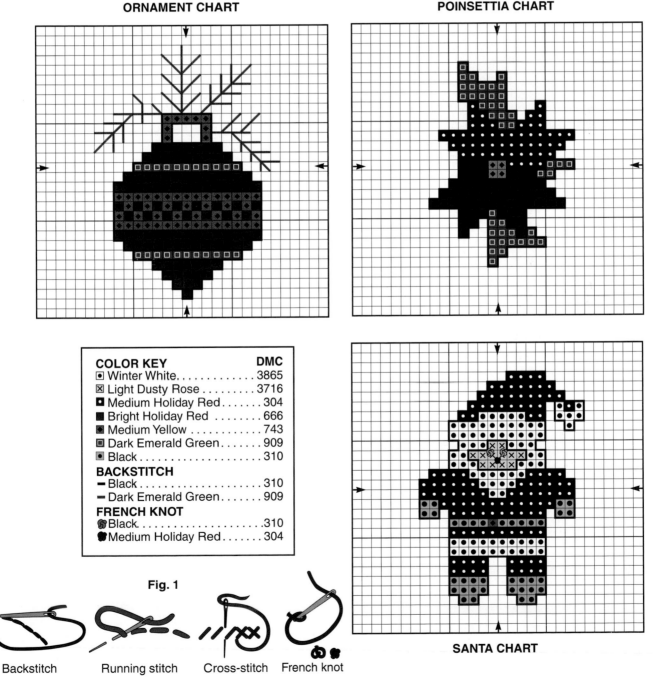

**ORNAMENT CHART**

**POINSETTIA CHART**

**COLOR KEY**         **DMC**
⊡ Winter White . . . . . . . . . . . . 3865
☒ Light Dusty Rose . . . . . . . . . 3716
◪ Medium Holiday Red . . . . . . 304
◼ Bright Holiday Red . . . . . . . 666
⊛ Medium Yellow . . . . . . . . . . . 743
▣ Dark Emerald Green . . . . . . 909
⊙ Black . . . . . . . . . . . . . . . . . . 310

**BACKSTITCH**
— Black . . . . . . . . . . . . . . . . . . 310
— Dark Emerald Green . . . . . . 909

**FRENCH KNOT**
❀ Black . . . . . . . . . . . . . . . . . . 310
❀ Medium Holiday Red . . . . . . 304

**Fig. 1**

Backstitch     Running stitch     Cross-stitch   French knot

**SANTA CHART**

# *Gingerbread House Keeps Special Treats*

GIVE A HOME to Christmas recipe cards with this decorated papier-mache box. "It's a creative gift idea for just about anyone on your list," notes Sandy Rollinger of Apollo, Pennsylvania.

**MATERIALS NEEDED:**
5-3/4-inch-wide x 7-1/2-inch-high x 3-3/4-inch-deep papier-mache house-shaped box
Oven-bake polymer clay (Sandy used Sculpey)—Poppy and Whipped Cream
Clay roller
Clay slicer
Plastic mat for rolling clay
Water container
Paper towels
Foam plate or palette
Acrylic craft paints (Sandy used FolkArt)—Apple Orchard, Sunny Yellow, Teddy Bear Brown and Tickled Pink
Paintbrushes—3/4-inch wash and No. 12 shader
Dimensional paints (Sandy used Plaid Outdoor)—Engine Red, Hot Pink and two bottles of Wicker White
Circle cutters—1-inch and 3/4-inch
Multicolored seed beads
1-1/2-inch-high gingerbread man cookie cutter
Foil-covered baking sheet
Oven
Pencil
Ruler
Craft glue

**FINISHED SIZE:** House recipe box measures about 7-1/2 inches high x 5-3/4 inches wide x 3-3/4 inches deep.

**DIRECTIONS:**
Refer to the photo at left as a guide while assembling house as directed in the instructions that follow.

CLAY: Condition clay and roll it to a 1/8-inch thickness on plastic mat.

From Whipped Cream clay, cut 32 circles using 3/4-inch circle cutter for shingles on roof. Use 1-inch circle cutter to cut a circle for dormer window and use cookie cutter to cut two gingerbread men.

Also from Whipped Cream clay, cut a 2-inch-high x 1-1/2-inch-wide rounded door and cut eight 1-inch squares. Cut four of the squares in half for shutters, leaving four squares for windows.

Roll a 1/2-inch-thick x 5-inch-long log of Whipped Cream clay. Roll a same-size log of Poppy clay and place the two logs side-by-side. Twist and roll them together to form a spiral pattern that resembles a peppermint stick. Continue to roll the log to a 1/2-inch thickness. Cut the log in half crosswise. Trim each piece as needed to fit against the front corners of the house.

Repeat to make two more peppermint sticks for the back corners of house.

Roll a 1/2-inch-thick x 3-inch-long log of Whipped Cream clay. Roll a same-size log of Poppy clay and place the two logs side-by-side. Twist and roll them together to form a spiral pattern as before. Continue to roll the log to a 1/4-inch thickness. Use slicer to cut thirty 1/4-inch-thick disks for peppermint candies on the sides of chimney.

Roll the remaining portion of log to make a 1/8-inch-thick log. Cut one length to form trim around door.

Place all clay shapes on foil-lined baking sheet. Shape door trim to fit around door, but do not let trim touch edges of door. Bake clay shapes at 275° for about 30 minutes. Let shapes cool in oven before removing.

PAINTING: Keep paper towels and water handy to clean paintbrushes. Place dabs of each paint color on a foam plate or palette as needed. Add coats of paint as needed for complete coverage. Let the paint dry after every application.

Remove lid from house box. Use wash brush and Teddy Bear Brown to paint entire outside of box and lid.

Use shader and Teddy Bear Brown to paint clay door, windows and shutters.

For shingles, use shader to paint 12 of the 3/4-inch clay circles Apple Orchard, 10 of the circles Sunny Yellow and 10 of the circles Tickled Pink.

Use pencil to draw a wavy line around the house about 1 inch down from the top. Use Hot Pink dimensional paint to paint over the line.

Use Engine Red and Wicker White dimensional paints to add dots in alternating colors along both sides of pink line.

Glue door, windows, shutters, peppermint stick corner pieces and gingerbread men to house.

Glue painted shingles to the top of roof, leaving about 1/4 inch between shingles.

Glue the peppermint candy pieces to the sides of chimney, leaving a small space between pieces. Let dry.

Use Hot Pink dimensional paint to add wavy lines around the door, windows and shutters.

Use Engine Red dimensional paint to add a mouth and small heart to each gingerbread man. Add a small heart to each shutter and the door. Add a small dot to door for doorknob.

Use Wicker White dimensional paint to add two tiny dots to each gingerbread man for eyes. Add wavy lines to the arms, legs and head.

Use Wicker White dimensional paint to cover the roof of the dormer. While paint is still wet, sprinkle roof of dormer with seed beads.

Add Wicker White dimensional paint to the center of each window and sprinkle on beads as before. In the same way, add Wicker White paint and beads to the bottom edge of house, to the top of chimney and to the tops of peppermint sticks at corners.

Add Wicker White dimensional paint to the tops of all windows and shutters. Add Wicker White dimensional paint to the spaces between the roof shingles and between the peppermint candies on chimney.

Add alternating dots of Engine Red and Wicker White dimensional paint around the window on the dormer.

Use Wicker White dimensional paint to add icicles to the edges of the roof and dormer. Let dry. ❄

# Toast the Holidays With Beaded Charms

*SERVE UP extra cheer with the Christmas light charms from Nancy Valentine Baker of Paupack, Pennsylvania. Add one to each wine glass so your guests can easily identify their own.*

**MATERIALS NEEDED** (for one):
Beading chart on this page
14-inch length of 28-gauge gold wire
Nineteen 4mm round transparent beads (aqua, green, pink, purple or red)
Six 3mm round gold metallic beads
Gold wire earring hoop
Wire cutters

**FINISHED SIZE:** Excluding gold loop, each beaded charm measures about 1-1/4 inches long x 5/8 inch wide.

**DIRECTIONS** (for one):
Fold the gold wire in half and center a 4mm bead on it to start the first row at the bottom of the lightbulb. See beading chart below right.

Add two more 4mm beads to one wire end and insert the other wire end through the same two beads, crossing the wire ends through the beads. Pull both wire ends taut, keeping them of equal length.

Referring to beading chart, continue adding rows of 4mm beads in the same way until you have added all nineteen 4mm beads as shown.

Add a row of three 3mm gold beads the same as before.

Add a gold bead to each wire end, leaving the ends uncrossed. Then add another gold bead by crossing both wire ends through it, completing the top row of gold beads.

Twist the wire ends together above the top beaded row, leaving a small space between the wires and the center bead. Clip excess wire.

Slide the twisted wire end of beaded lightbulb onto the gold wire hoop. Close hoop around stem of glass. ❄

**BEADING CHART**

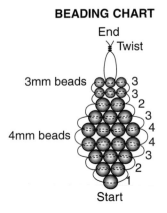

Tuck the bottom triangle between layers of the open edge. Turn the folded triangle over. Fold left point of triangle over to the bottom right as shown in Fig. 3, forming the stand back. Crease fold as before. Turn place marker over.

Trace star pattern onto folded tracing paper with pencil. Cut out star along outline and open for complete pattern.

Cut star from patterned card stock. Glue star to upper left side of stand. Adhere stickers where desired. Let dry.

Slip left edge of name card into front fold of stand. ❂

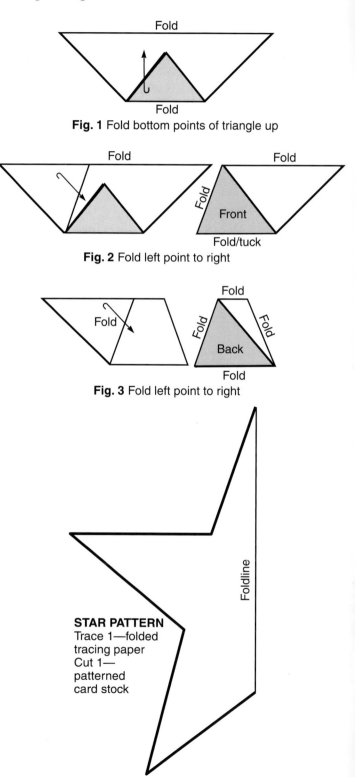

**Fig. 1** Fold bottom points of triangle up

**Fig. 2** Fold left point to right

**Fig. 3** Fold left point to right

# Starry Place Card Will Delight Guests

*THE SKY'S THE LIMIT with this origami project from Lenora Schut of Pella, Iowa. She folded a simple stand and attached a star...but you could add any shape you like, or even a photo.*

MATERIALS NEEDED (for one):
Patterns on this page
Tracing paper and pencil
Green solid card stock—6-inch square and a 2-1/2-inch x 3-inch rectangle for name card
Patterned card stock for trim on name card
5-inch square of patterned card stock for star
Folding tool
Black permanent marker for writing name
Assorted stickers for decorations
Pop Dots (optional)
Craft glue
Ruler
Scissors

FINISHED SIZE: Excluding name card, star place marker measures about 3-3/4 inches high x 4 inches wide.

DIRECTIONS (for one):
NAME CARD: For trim, cut a 3-inch x 3/4-inch strip from patterned card stock.

With edges matching, glue patterned strip to one long edge of the 2-1/2-inch x 3-inch green card stock rectangle.

Using black marker, write a guest's name below the patterned strip on green card stock. Let dry.

STAR PLACE MARKER: Fold 6-inch square of green card stock in half diagonally to make a triangle. Crease fold with folding tool.

Place folded triangle on a flat surface with the fold at the top. Referring to Fig. 1 above right, fold up bottom points to about 3/4 inch from top fold. Crease fold as before.

Fold left point of triangle over to the bottom right as shown in Fig. 2, forming the stand front. Crease fold as before.

**STAR PATTERN**
Trace 1—folded tracing paper
Cut 1—patterned card stock

Foldline

# Pamper Pets with A Gift of Treats

*ARE FURRY FRIENDS on your gift list? Wrap animal snacks with these clever bags from Loretta Mateik, Petaluma, California. Turn to page 63 to find a recipe for homemade dog biscuits!*

MATERIALS NEEDED (for both):
Patterns on this page
Tracing paper and pencil
Black fine-line marker
Two clear cellophane bags for pet treats (Loretta used 3-inch x 8-1/2-inch bags)
Stapler
Craft glue
Scissors
(For cat):
Card stock—4-inch square of red, 2-inch x 3-inch rectangle of gold and 1/2-inch square of pink
Cat treats
(For dog):
Card stock—4-inch square of light green, 3-inch x 4-inch rectangle of tan and 1-inch square of black
Markers—brown medium-point and white opaque
Dog treats

FINISHED SIZE: Cat treat bag measures about 4 inches long x 2-3/4 inches wide. Dog treat bag measures about 4 inches long x 3 inches wide.

DIRECTIONS:
Trace patterns separately onto tracing paper with pencil. Cut out shapes.

CAT: Place cat treats inside cellophane bag. Fold top down and staple bag closed.

Fold red square of card stock in half to make a rectangle for bag topper.

Trace cat head pattern onto gold card stock. Trace cat nose pattern onto pink card stock. Cut out shapes.

Referring to the photo at right as a guide, use black marker to add details to head and nose.

Glue nose to head.

Referring to photo for position, glue cat to red rectangle. Let dry.

Using black marker, write "For:" and cat's name on red rectangle.

Place folded bag topper over the top of bag and glue in place. Let dry.

DOG: Place dog treats inside cellophane bag. Fold top down and staple bag closed.

Fold light green square of card stock in half to make a rectangle for bag topper.

Trace dog ear and head patterns onto tan card stock. Trace dog nose pattern onto black card stock. Cut out shapes.

Referring to photo as a guide, use black marker to outline dog's head and ears and to add the eyebrows, eyes and mouth.

Using brown marker, add spots to head and ears.

Using white marker, add highlight to top of nose and add a tiny dot to each eye.

Glue ears to opposite sides on back of head. Glue nose to front of head.

Referring to photo for position, glue dog to light green rectangle. Let dry.

Use black marker to write "For:" and dog's name on light green rectangle.

Place folded bag topper over the top of bag and glue in place. Let dry. ❄

## PET TREAT HOLDER PATTERNS
Trace 1 each—tracing paper

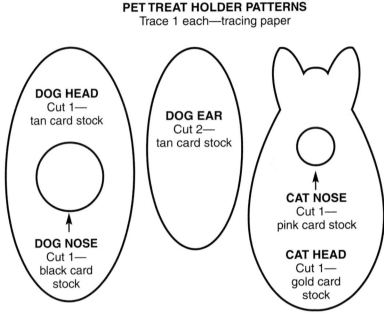

DOG HEAD
Cut 1—
tan card stock

DOG EAR
Cut 2—
tan card stock

DOG NOSE
Cut 1—
black card stock

CAT NOSE
Cut 1—
pink card stock

CAT HEAD
Cut 1—
gold card stock

# Give Little Cuties A Sweet Santa Hat

*ANY GIRL will want to be Santa's helper when wearing this fanciful cap from Cori Harrison of New Berlin, Wisconsin. She created furry white trim and attached a feathery hair clip.*

**MATERIALS NEEDED:**
One skein of red bulky yarn (Cori used Lion Brand
   Wool-Ease Thick & Quick yarn in Cranberry)
One skein of white super bulky yarn (Cori used Red
   Heart Light & Lofty yarn in Puff)
One skein of white eyelash novelty yarn (Cori used
   Patons Allure yarn in Diamond)
Red round Knifty Knitter loom set (see Editor's Note) or
   set of four size 13 double-pointed knitting needles (or
   size needed to obtain correct gauge)

Yarn or tapestry needle
Measuring tape
Scissors
20-inch length of white boa trim
White feather hair clip

**EDITOR'S NOTE:** Round Knifty Knitter loom sets are available in four sizes and can be found at many craft stores. Cori used the red round Knifty Knitter.

**GAUGE:** Working on size 13 knitting needles, 7 sts and 14 rows = 4 inches.

**FINISHED SIZE:** Child-size hat has a circumference of about 18 inches.

**DIRECTIONS:**
Holding the white super bulky and white novelty yarns as one, either wrap the Knifty Knitter loom following the loom manufacturer's instructions, or cast on 31 sts evenly distributed onto three double-pointed needles; join without twisting to work in rounds.

Work 2 inches on loom following manufacturer's instructions, or k 2 inches on needles. Fasten off white yarns.

Attach red yarn. Work about 7 inches on loom or needles as before. Cut yarn, leaving a 20-inch tail.

Thread yarn end onto yarn or tapestry needle. Run the needle and yarn through the lps on each peg of the loom or on knitting needles. Remove the lps from the pegs or needles. Fasten off the yarn without drawing up the lps.

Thread yarn or tapestry needle with another 20-inch length of red yarn. Sew around hat about 2 inches from top with a long running stitch. Remove needle and draw up ends of yarn to gather and close top of hat. Tie yarn ends in a small bow.

Thread white boa trim onto yarn or tapestry needle.

With long stitches, attach boa trim to top edge of white band. Fasten off and trim away excess.

Attach feather hair clip to hat where desired. ❋

| ABBREVIATIONS | | |
|---|---|---|
| k knit | lp(s) loop(s) | st(s) stitch(es) |

# Felt Claus Purse Has Fun in Hand

*LOOKING for a new way to use old buttons? Try this project from Mary Ayres of Boyce, Virginia. Fill the adorable handbag with treats for an extra-special Christmas gift.*

**MATERIALS NEEDED:**
Patterns on next page
Tracing paper and pencil
Size 8 black pearl cotton

Wool felt—1/4 yard of white for purse and inside of strap,
   1/8 yard of red for hat brim and outside of strap, and
   scrap of fleshtone for Santa's face
Embroidery needle
Approximately 45 white sew-through buttons in assorted
   sizes for hat brim
Two 5/8-inch pink sew-through buttons for cheeks
One 5/8-inch red sew-through button for purse strap
Two 3/8-inch black snaps for eyes
White all-purpose thread
Off-white cotton cord for pom-pom
1-1/4-inch x 5-inch piece of cardboard
Standard sewing supplies

**PATTERN KEY**
— Outline/cutting line
--- Inside design line
X Placement of snaps
● Placement of pink buttons

**Fig. 1** Blanket stitch

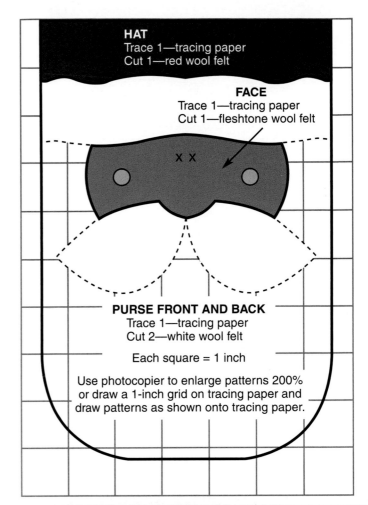

**HAT**
Trace 1—tracing paper
Cut 1—red wool felt

**FACE**
Trace 1—tracing paper
Cut 1—fleshtone wool felt

X X

**PURSE FRONT AND BACK**
Trace 1—tracing paper
Cut 2—white wool felt

Each square = 1 inch

Use photocopier to enlarge patterns 200%
or draw a 1-inch grid on tracing paper and
draw patterns as shown onto tracing paper.

FINISHED SIZE: Excluding strap, Santa bag measures about 9 inches high x 8 inches wide.

DIRECTIONS:
PREPARATION: Wet white, red and fleshtone wool felt with water separately. Dry each separately in dryer to give the felt a crinkly aged look.

Trace enlarged patterns onto tracing paper with pencil as directed on patterns.

Cut pattern pieces from felt as directed on patterns.

ASSEMBLY: Pin red hat and fleshtone face pieces to right side of one purse piece as shown on pattern.

Thread embroidery needle with a single strand of black pearl cotton. Blanket-stitch across the top and bottom of red hat piece and around edge of fleshtone face. See Fig. 1 above for stitch illustration.

With pencil, transfer inside design lines of hat and mustache to front of purse. Blanket-stitch along marked lines.

Using white thread, hand-sew black snaps and pink buttons to face where shown on pattern. Hand-sew assorted white buttons to hat brim, leaving about 1/4 inch along each side edge of brim uncovered for blanket stitches.

Pin front and back purse pieces together with wrong sides together. Blanket-stitch around edge of purse, leaving the top edge open.

For strap, cut a 1-inch x 14-inch strip each of white and red felt. Pin strips together with edges matching. Blanket-stitch around edges.

With red side out, pin opposite ends of strap to opposite top edges of purse. Hand-sew white side of strap ends to purse. With black pearl cotton, hand-sew red button to one strap end.

POM-POM: For the tie, cut a 10-inch length of cord. Center tie along the 5-inch length of the cardboard strip.

Working back and forth along the length of the cardboard strip, wrap cord around the tie and width of strip about 30 times so that each wrap is smooth but not tight and lies against the previous wrap.

Carefully bend the cardboard strip lengthwise and remove the cardboard without removing the tie.

Knot the ends of the tie with a double knot, pulling the ends tight to make a donut shape.

Without cutting the ends of the tie, cut loops along the outermost edge of donut shape. Fluff ends to untwist the cord. Trim ends even.

Hand-sew pom-pom to remaining end of purse strap. ❀

# Cheery Cards Bring The Holidays Home

*OPEN THE DOOR to Christmas fun with these charming cards. "I love making my own because it adds a personal touch and gives me a chance to be creative," says Mary Ayres of Boyce, Virginia.*

**MATERIALS NEEDED** (for both):

Patterns on next page
Tracing paper and pencil
Heavy-weight patterned papers (Mary used Basic Grey paper)—yellow, textured red, damask red, lime green, bright green, coordinating stripe and white
Ink pads—blue, green, red and yellow
White card stock
Four gold brads
Four 12-inch lengths of red pearl cotton
Black markers—fine-line and medium-point
Iridescent glitter
Small paintbrush and craft glue for paper
Ruler
Scissors—straight and scallop
Circle punches—1/16-inch, 1/8-inch, 1/4-inch and 3/4-inch
Scoring blade

**FINISHED SIZE:** Tall house card measures about 5-1/2 inches high x 4-1/4 inches across. Wide house card measures about 4-1/4 inches high x 5-1/2 inches across.

**DIRECTIONS:**

Trace enlarged patterns separately onto tracing paper with pencil. Cut out shapes following outline of patterns.

**GENERAL INSTRUCTIONS:** Before gluing the cutout paper pieces together, shade the outside edges of each piece, except the tags, with the following ink colors:

Rub red ink on red paper pieces, yellow ink on yellow pieces, green ink on green pieces and blue ink on white and striped pieces.

**TALL HOUSE: Card:** Cut an 8-1/2-inch x 5-1/2-inch rectangle from white card stock.

Score a line crosswise across the center of the white rectangle and fold it in half to make a 5-1/2-inch-tall x 4-1/4-inch-wide card.

**Front:** Cut a 5-1/2-inch x 4-1/4-inch piece of red patterned paper. With edges matching, glue the red paper to the front of card. With the fold of the card at the left, place the tall house pattern on top of card and trim the top of card following the roof line on pattern.

**Roof trim:** Cut two 1/2-inch-wide x 4-inch-long strips of white card stock. Trim one long edge of each strip with scal-

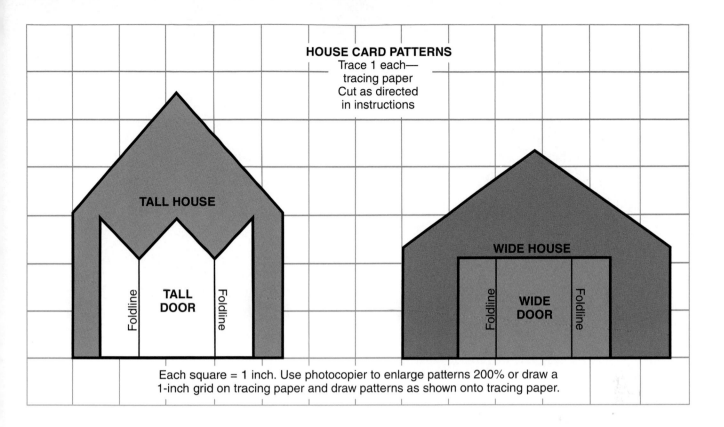

**HOUSE CARD PATTERNS**
Trace 1 each—
tracing paper
Cut as directed
in instructions

TALL HOUSE

TALL DOOR

Foldline

Foldline

WIDE HOUSE

WIDE DOOR

Foldline

Foldline

Each square = 1 inch. Use photocopier to enlarge patterns 200% or draw a 1-inch grid on tracing paper and draw patterns as shown onto tracing paper.

lop scissors to make a 3/8-inch-wide strip with an inverted scallop.

Glue roof trim to top edges of roof. Trim short ends of trim even with edges of card.

**Door and windows:** Place tall door pattern on wrong side of striped paper and cut out door. With the striped pattern on the outside, fold sides of door in where foldlines are shown on pattern.

Cut traced door pattern along foldlines to create pattern for inner door piece.

From yellow paper, cut one inner door piece, two 3/4-inch x 2-1/4-inch rectangles for side windows and one 1-inch square for dormer window.

Glue inner door piece right side up to inside center of door. Let dry.

Referring to the photo above left, use fine-line marker to add design lines to windows. Use medium-point marker to write "holiday hugs to you" on inner door piece.

Open sides of door and use fine-line marker to outline each inside door section.

Use 1/8-inch circle punch to make a hole in each side of door for doorknobs. Insert a gold brad into each hole and bend prongs on the inside.

**Wreath:** Use circle punch to cut a 3/4-inch circle from bright green patterned paper. Punch a 1/4-inch hole in the center of the 3/4-inch circle to make a wreath. Glue wreath to center of square window.

**Tag:** Cut a 1-1/4-inch x 1/2-inch rectangle from white card stock. At one short end of rectangle, cut off the corners to create a tag shape.

Use fine-line marker to write "Please Enter" and to add a border around the edge.

Use 1/16-inch punch to make a hole at the narrow end.

**Finishing:** Referring to photo for position, glue assembled door and windows to front of card.

Wrap a length of red pearl cotton around brads on door and add the tag. Tie ends in a bow to close doors. Trim ends of bow as desired. Tie an overhand knot close to each end.

Tie another length of red pearl cotton into a small bow. Trim ends as desired. Glue bow to top of wreath.

Use paintbrush to apply a thin layer of glue to roof trim and windowpanes. While glue is still wet, sprinkle on glitter. Let dry. Tap off excess glitter when dry.

**WIDE HOUSE: Card:** Cut an 11-inch x 4-1/4-inch rectangle from white card stock.

Score a line crosswise across the center of the white rectangle and fold it in half to make a 4-1/4-inch-high x 5-1/2-inch-wide card.

**Front:** Cut a 4-1/4-inch x 5-1/2-inch piece of lime green patterned paper. With edges matching, glue the green paper to the front of the card. With the fold of the card at the left, place the wide house pattern on top of card and trim the top of card following roof line on pattern.

**Roof trim:** Follow instructions for tall house card.

**Door:** Follow instructions for tall house card, using damask red patterned paper instead of striped paper.

**Windows:** Follow instructions for tall house card, cutting 1-inch x 1-1/2-inch rectangles for side windows.

**Wreath and tag:** Follow instructions for tall house card.

**Finishing:** Follow instructions for tall house card. ❈

# Quilted Floor Pillow Will Keep You Comfy

*BIG AND COZY, this floor pillow is sure to beckon your holiday guests—even if there are plenty of chairs to go around! Country Woman Craft Editor Jane Craig created the festive design.*

**MATERIALS NEEDED:**
44-inch-wide 100% cotton fabrics—3/4 yard of red floral print for blocks; 2 yards of green print for sashing, outer pillow flange and envelope pillow back; and 1/4 yard of small red print for binding
All-purpose thread to match fabrics
32-inch square of fabric for backing
32-inch square of lightweight quilt batting
Rotary cutting tools
Quilter's ruler
27-inch square pillow form
Standard sewing supplies

**FINISHED SIZE:** Pillow is about 33 inches square.

**DIRECTIONS:**
Wash all fabrics, washing each color separately. If rinse water is discolored, wash again until water runs clear.

Dry and press fabrics.

CUTTING: Referring to Fig. 1 at far right and using rotary cutter and quilter's ruler, accurately cut fabrics as follows:

From red floral print, cut thirteen 6-inch squares (A). Cut two 9-inch squares, then cut these squares in half twice diagonally to make eight triangles for sides (B). Cut two 4-3/4-inch squares, then cut these squares in half diagonally to make four triangles for corners (C).

From green print, cut thirty-six 1-1/2-inch x 6-inch rectangles for sashing (D) and twelve 1-1/2-inch squares for corners (E). Cut three 2-5/8-inch squares, then cut these squares in half diagonally twice to make 12 triangles for sides (F). Cut eight 3-inch x 44-inch strips and eight 3-inch squares for outer flange on front and back of pillow. For envelope pillow

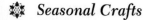

back, cut two 21-1/2-inch x 27-1/2-inch rectangles.

From small red print, cut four 2-1/2-inch x 44-inch strips for binding.

**PIECING:** Do all piecing with right sides of fabrics together, edges matching and an accurate 1/4-inch seam.

Referring to Fig. 1 and layout diagram below, lay out pieces A through F right side up on a flat surface.

Sew a small triangle (F) to opposite short ends of one sashing rectangle (D). Press seams in one direction. Sew assembled sashing strip to the long edge of a corner triangle (C). Press seam toward sashing strip.

Sew a side triangle (B), sashing rectangle (D), square (A), sashing rectangle (D) and side triangle (B) together as shown. Press seams in opposite direction. Sew assembled row to bottom of previous row.

In the same way, sew remaining pieces and rows together to form the pillow top.

**QUILTING:** Place backing fabric on a flat surface. Center batting on top of backing. Center pieced pillow top right side up on top of batting.

Baste layers together as needed to hold.

Quilt as desired.

Trim excess batting and back, squaring the top.

**PILLOW BACK:** Press one long edge of each 21-1/2-inch x 27-1/2-inch pillow back piece 1/4 inch to wrong side. Fold and press 1 inch to wrong side and sew close to first fold with matching thread for hem.

Place pillow back pieces right side up on back of pieced and quilted pillow top with outside edges matching and hemmed edges of pillow back pieces overlapping.

Pin to hold and sew around outside edges with a scant 1/4-inch seam.

**FLANGE:** Cut the eight 3-inch-wide pieces of green print equal to the length of sides of the pillow top for the flange.

Pin a flange piece to both the front and back of one side of the pillow top with raw edges matching. (The pillow top will be sandwiched between the flange pieces.) Sew the edge with a 1/4-inch seam. Open and press. Repeat on opposite side of pillow top.

Sew a 3-inch square to opposite short ends of each remaining flange piece. Pin and sew a pieced flange strip to front and back of top edge of pillow top as before. Repeat on bottom edge of pillow top. Open and press.

Baste flange edges together with wrong sides together and edges matching.

**BINDING:** Sew short ends of binding strips together diagonally to make one long strip. Trim and press seams open.

Press one short end diagonally 1/4 inch to wrong side.

Press strip in half lengthwise with wrong sides together.

Sew binding strip to right side of pillow flange with edges matching and a 1/4-inch seam, mitering corners.

Fold binding to back, encasing raw edges.

Hand-sew fold of binding to back of pillow flange, covering seam. Insert pillow form. ❄

**Fig. 1** Piecing diagonal rows

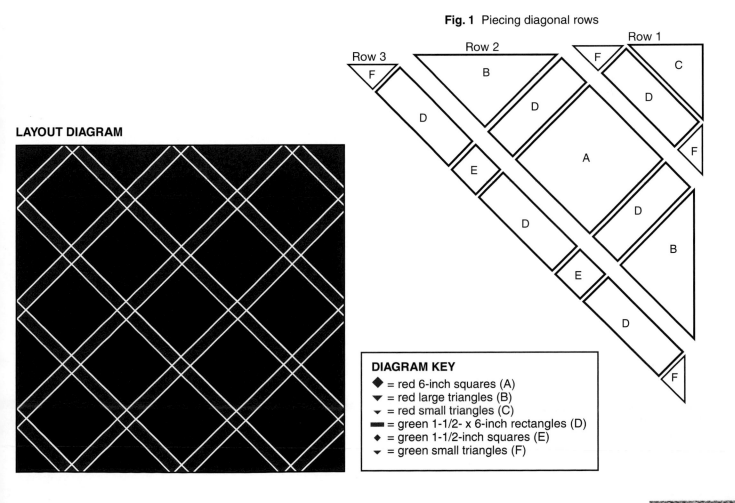

**LAYOUT DIAGRAM**

**DIAGRAM KEY**
◆ = red 6-inch squares (A)
▼ = red large triangles (B)
▾ = red small triangles (C)
▬ = green 1-1/2- x 6-inch rectangles (D)
◆ = green 1-1/2-inch squares (E)
▾ = green small triangles (F)

# Beaded Snowflakes Add Noel Sparkle

*JUST LIKE Mother Nature, you can make your own one-of-a-kind snowflakes. The Country Woman staff simply strung pretty beads onto a wire snowflake form available at bead stores.*

**MATERIALS NEEDED** (for one):
Snowflake ornament wire form (the *CW* staff used a 4-1/2-inch Beadsmith form)
Assorted beads of your choice (the *CW* staff used Bead Heaven Classic Glass beads)—Crystal & Ruby, Light Sapphire & Light Amethyst, and Sapphire
Needle-nose pliers or jewelry glue
6-inch length of monofilament thread for hanging loop

**FINISHED SIZE:** Excluding hanging loop, each beaded snowflake measures about 4-1/2 inches across.

**DIRECTIONS** (for one):
If desired, use Crystal & Ruby beads for a red snowflake, Light Sapphire & Light Amethyst beads for a purple snowflake or Sapphire beads for a blue snowflake.

Slip desired beads on a wire spoke of the wire ornament form, placing smaller beads at the center and adding more beads in the desired order.

Either glue the last bead onto the wire and let it dry, or leave a small section of unbeaded wire at the end of the spoke and use needle-nose pliers to make a very small loop at the end of the wire.

Use wire cutters to trim away any excess wire at the end of the spoke.

Add desired beads to the remaining wire spokes of the ornament in the same way.

Insert one end of monofilament thread through a wire loop or bead at the end of any spoke.

Tie the ends of the monofilament thread together to form a hanging loop. ❄

---

# Manger Scene Has Christmas Spirit

*CELEBRATE the reason for the season with this beautiful cross-stitch from Ronda Bryce of North Augusta, South Carolina. Unlike more elaborate designs, it won't take long to create.*

**MATERIALS NEEDED:**
Chart on next page
Three 12-inch squares of off-white 14-count Aida cloth
DMC six-strand embroidery floss in colors listed on color key
Size 24 tapestry needle
Scissors

**FINISHED SIZE:** Design area is 60 stitches high x 55 stitches wide and measures 4-1/4 inches high x 3-7/8 inches wide.

**DIRECTIONS:**
Zigzag or overcast the edges of the Aida cloth piece to prevent fraying. To find the center of the Aida cloth piece, fold it in half crosswise, then fold it in half lengthwise and mark where the folds intersect.

Draw lines across the chart, connecting opposite arrows.

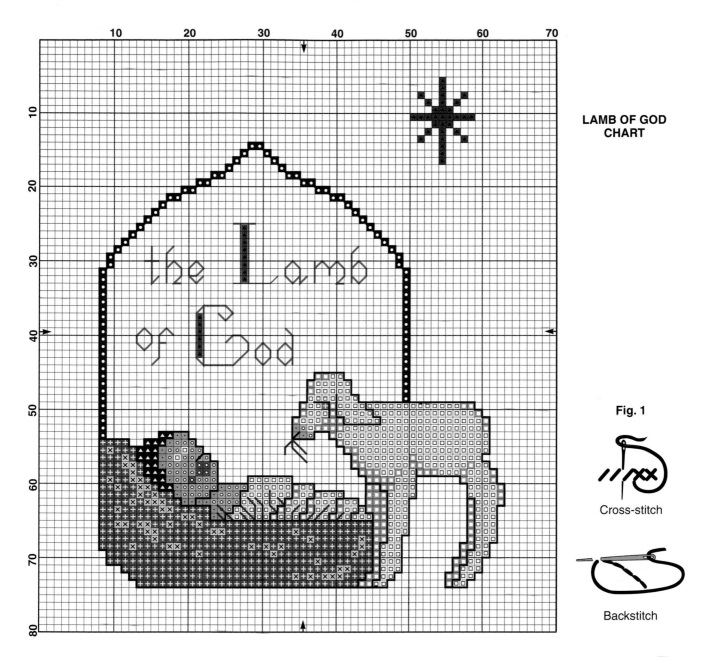

**LAMB OF GOD CHART**

**Fig. 1**

Cross-stitch

Backstitch

Mark where the lines intersect. Begin stitching here for a centered design.

Each square on the chart represents one set of fabric threads surrounded by four holes. Each stitch is worked over one set of threads with the needle passing through the holes.

The color and/or symbol inside each square on the chart, along with the color key, indicates which color of six-strand embroidery floss to use to make the cross-stitches. Wide lines on the chart show where to make backstitches. See Fig. 1 above right for stitch illustrations.

Use 18-inch lengths of floss. Longer strands tend to tangle and fray. Separate the strands of floss and thread the needle with two strands for all cross-stitches. Use one strand for backstitches.

To begin stitching, leave a 1-inch tail of floss on the back of the design and hold tail in place while working the first few stitches over it. To end stitching, run needle under a few stitches in back before clipping the floss close to work.

When all stitching is complete, and only if necessary, gently wash the stitched piece in lukewarm water. Press right side down on a terry-cloth towel to dry.

Frame stitched piece as desired. ❋

| COLOR KEY | DMC |
|---|---|
| ◩ Medium Navy Blue | 311 |
| ☒ Pewter Gray | 317 |
| ☐ Pearl Gray | 415 |
| ▣ Light Peach | 754 |
| ◨ Salmon | 760 |
| ▲ Dark Coffee Brown | 801 |
| ⊙ Very Light Peach | 948 |
| ⊞ Very Dark Pewter Gray | 3799 |
| ▢ Winter White | 3865 |
| ■ Metallic Gold | 5282 |
| **BACKSTITCH** | |
| — Black | 310 |
| — Medium Navy Blue | 311 |
| — Light Brown | 434 |

# Christmas Ornament Quilt Warms Hearts

*IF YOU LOVE to quilt but don't have lots of time, try this delightful design. "It was simple to make and brightens up my decor for the holidays," says Loretta Mateik of Petaluma, California.*

## MATERIALS NEEDED:

Patterns on next page
Tracing paper and pencil
Paper-backed fusible web
44-inch-wide 100% cotton fabrics—1/2 yard of
   green-on-white print for background and outer border,
   1/8 yard of light green print for ornament and outer
   border, 1/6 yard of dark green print for ornament and
   outer border, 1/8 yard of red stripe for ornament and
   outer border, 1/8 yard of holly print for outer corners,
   1/8 yard of green solid for inner border, 1/8 yard of
   gold solid for binding and orament tops, and 1 yard of
   coordinating fabric for backing and hanging sleeve
28-inch x 30-inch piece of lightweight quilt batting
All-purpose thread to match fabrics
Six-strand embroidery floss—dark green, gold, light
   green and red
Embroidery needle
Quilter's marking pen or pencil
Quilter's ruler
Rotary cutter and mat
Standard sewing supplies

**FINISHED SIZE:** Wall hanging measures about 26-1/2 inches high x 24-1/2 inches wide.

## DIRECTIONS:

**CUTTING:** Cut fabrics using rotary cutter and quilter's ruler as follows:

From green-on-white print, cut one 13-1/2-inch x 15-1/2-inch piece for background and one 4-1/2-inch-wide x 16-inch-long crosswise strip for outer border.

From light green print, cut one 4-1/2-inch-wide x 16-inch-long crosswise strip for outer border.

From dark green print, cut two 4-1/2-inch-wide x 16-inch-long crosswise strips for outer border.

From red stripe, cut one 4-1/2-inch-wide x 16-inch-long crosswise strip for outer border.

From holly print, cut four 3-1/2-inch squares for outer corners.

From green solid, cut two 3-inch x 15-1/2-inch strips and two 3-inch x 18-1/2-inch strips for inner border.

From gold solid, cut four 2-1/2-inch-wide crosswise strips for binding.

From backing fabric, cut one 28-inch x 30-inch piece for backing and one 3-inch x 24-inch strip for hanging sleeve.

**PIECING:** Do all stitching with right sides of fabrics together, edges even, matching thread and an accurate 1/4-inch seam. Press seams toward the darker fabric.

**Inner border:** Sew a 3-inch x 15-1/2-inch green solid strip to each long edge of background piece. Open and press.

Sew a 3-inch x 18-1/2-inch green solid strip to top and bottom of background piece. Open and press.

**Outer border:** Sew long edges of the 16-inch outer border strips together in the following order: dark green print, red stripe, green-on-white print, light green print and another dark green print. Press seams toward darker fabrics.

From this stitched piece, cut four 3-1/2-inch-wide pieced strips. Sew one pieced strip to each long side of inner border. Open and press seams toward borders.

Trim dark green rectangles on each end of remaining pieced strips to 3-1/2-inch x 3-1/4-inch rectangles to fit the top and bottom inner border edges. Sew a 3-1/2-inch holly print square to opposite ends of each pieced strip.

Sew a pieced strip to the top and bottom edges of inner border. Open and press seams toward borders.

**APPLIQUE:** Trace enlarged patterns separately onto tracing paper. Cut out.

Trace around patterns onto paper side of fusible web, leaving at least 1/2 inch between shapes. Cut apart shapes, leaving a margin of paper around each.

Following web manufacturer's instructions, fuse shapes onto wrong side of fabrics as directed on patterns. Cut out shapes following outline of patterns. Remove paper backing from shapes.

Referring to photo above left for position, fuse the ornaments and then the gold tops to the background piece, overlapping the pieces as shown on the patterns.

**EMBROIDERY:** Using a quilter's pen or pencil, write "Season's" centered in the top inner border. Write "Greetings" centered in the bottom inner border and draw a straight line and circle above each ornament.

Separate six-strand floss and thread embroidery needle

with two strands of floss for all stitching in the instructions that follow. See Fig. 1 below right for stitch illustrations.

Chain-stitch over marked lettering with gold floss.

Blanket-stitch around ornaments with coordinating floss and around ornament tops with gold floss.

Chain-stitch along marked straight lines and circles with green floss.

QUILTING: Place backing fabric wrong side up on a flat surface. Center batting on top of backing. Center pieced top right side up on batting and smooth out all wrinkles.

Baste layers together. Hand- or machine-quilt as desired.

Machine-stitch 1/8 inch from outer edges of pieced top. Remove basting.

BINDING: Sew short ends of binding strips together diagonally to make one long strip. Trim and press seams open.

Press one short end diagonally 1/4 inch to wrong side.

Press strip in half lengthwise with wrong sides together.

Sew binding strip to right side of pieced top with edges matching and a 1/4-inch seam, mitering corners.

Fold binding to back, encasing raw edges.

Hand-sew fold of binding to back of quilt, covering seam.

HANGING SLEEVE: Hem short edges of 3-inch x 24-inch hanging sleeve piece.

Fold hanging sleeve in half lengthwise with wrong sides together. Sew long edges together with a narrow seam to make a tube. Press tube flat and seam open.

Pin hanging sleeve centered along top back of wall hanging.

Hand-sew folds of hanging sleeve to backing. ❄

**Fig. 1**

Chain stitch          Blanket stitch

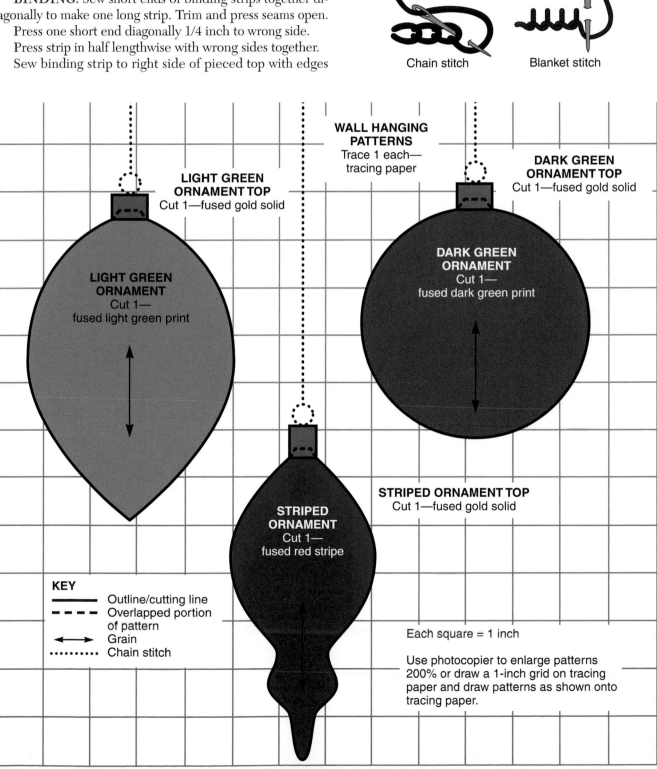

WALL HANGING PATTERNS
Trace 1 each— tracing paper

LIGHT GREEN ORNAMENT TOP
Cut 1—fused gold solid

DARK GREEN ORNAMENT TOP
Cut 1—fused gold solid

LIGHT GREEN ORNAMENT
Cut 1— fused light green print

DARK GREEN ORNAMENT
Cut 1— fused dark green print

STRIPED ORNAMENT TOP
Cut 1—fused gold solid

STRIPED ORNAMENT
Cut 1— fused red stripe

KEY
——— Outline/cutting line
- - - Overlapped portion of pattern
←→ Grain
········· Chain stitch

Each square = 1 inch

Use photocopier to enlarge patterns 200% or draw a 1-inch grid on tracing paper and draw patterns as shown onto tracing paper.

# Roll Out a Claus From the Kitchen

*TURNING an ordinary item into something special is easy with this painted St. Nick. "It's a fun way to put an artistic spin on an old rolling pin," says Irene Wegener of Corning, New York.*

## MATERIALS NEEDED:
Pattern on next page
Tracing paper and pencil
Graphite paper
Stylus or dry ballpoint pen
Wood rolling pin (Irene used a 20-inch-long rolling pin)
Scroll or band saw (or wood dowel and wood glue—see Preparation)
Drill with 1/8-inch bit
Purchased 1/2-inch-thick x 4-inch-wide wood circle for base
Finishing sandpaper
Water container
Paper towels
Foam plate or palette
Acrylic craft paints (Irene used Delta Ceramcoat and DecoArt Americana paints)—Antique Gold, Antique White, Asphaltum, Black, Black Cherry, Blush, Drizzle Grey, Fleshtone, Honey Brown and Pine Green
Paintbrushes—small flat, 1/4-inch angle brush and liner
1-inch sponge brush
Toothpick
Matte sealer
3-inch-long flat-headed wood screw and screwdriver
Natural or colored excelsior
Metal measuring spoon
Old-fashioned cookie cutters—4-inch-long tree and 2-inch-long holly
Two 3-inch-tall pre-painted wooden or resin gingerbread men or decorated gingerbread cookies
Three 1-inch artificial gumdrop star candies
Artificial holly leaves and three red berries
Glue gun and glue stick
Ruler

**FINISHED SIZE:** Including circle base, rolling pin Santa shown is about 16-1/2 inches high x 4 inches wide.

## DIRECTIONS:
**PREPARATION:** If your rolling pin has a metal rod that extends into the handles, remove one handle and the metal rod. Replace the rod with a wooden dowel that extends beyond the top to hold the remaining handle in place. Using wood glue, glue the dowel inside the rolling pin, then glue the handle onto the extending dowel. Let dry.

If you are using a one-piece rolling pin, use a scroll or band saw to remove one handle, leaving a flat surface to attach to the wood base.

Referring to Fig. 1 at right, drill a pilot hole into the end of the rolling pin without the handle and drill through the wood circle base.

Sand wood pieces smooth and wipe with a damp paper

towel to remove sanding dust.

PAINTING: Keep paper towels and a container of water handy to clean paintbrushes. Place dabs of each color of paint onto foam plate or palette as needed. Add coats of paint as needed for complete coverage. Let paint dry after every application. Refer to the photo at far left as a guide while painting as directed in the instructions that follow.

Use sponge brush and Black Cherry to paint the entire rolling pin.

In same way, paint entire wood circle base Pine Green.

Use flat brush and Antique White to paint a 1-inch-wide band around handle end of rolling pin for fur on Santa's hat.

Trace pattern onto tracing paper with pencil. Place pattern on rolling pin with top edge of pattern along lower edge of fur on hat. Slip graphite paper between pattern and rolling pin. Trace over pattern lines with stylus or dry ballpoint pen, transferring pattern onto rolling pin.

Use flat brush and Fleshtone to paint face.

Use flat brush and Drizzle Grey to paint beard.

Dip flat brush into Antique White and wipe excess paint onto a paper towel. With a nearly dry brush, apply Antique White over the beard, allowing some of the Drizzle Grey to show through. Also paint top of rolling pin handle.

Use flat brush and Drizzle Grey to paint mustache.

Use flat brush and Antique White to paint over mustache the same as for beard, allowing Drizzle Grey to show through and leaving a narrow Drizzle Grey border around mustache.

Use the 1/4-inch angle brush to float Asphaltum around outer edge of Santa's face, including the top edge.

Dip end of paintbrush handle into Black and add two small dots to Santa's face for eyes. In same way, add seven dots down the front for buttons.

Use liner and Asphaltum to paint line at top of each eye.

Use angle brush and Asphaltum to add shadow of eyebrow above the left eye. Add the shadow of right eyebrow in the

same way, extending the line down the center of Santa's face to his mustache for nose.

Use liner and Antique White to add each eyebrow and wispy bangs across the top of Santa's face.

Dip toothpick into Antique White and add a tiny dot to each eye.

Dip flat brush into Black Cherry and wipe excess paint onto a paper towel. With a nearly dry brush and a circular motion, add cheeks.

Dip flat brush into Honey Brown and wipe excess paint onto a paper towel. With a nearly dry brush, apply Honey Brown over fur of hat, allowing the Antique White to show through.

Dip toothpick into Antique Gold and add two tiny dots to each button.

Apply sealer to rolling pin and base following manufacturer's instructions.

ASSEMBLY: Insert screw through hole in base from the bottom to the top, then into the pilot hole on bottom of rolling pin Santa. Tighten screw with screwdriver, positioning rolling pin so that Santa faces the wide area of base.

FINISHING: Using glue gun, glue excelsior around the top of the base.

Referring to photo for position, glue spoon, cookie cutters, gingerbread men and artificial candies to excelsior. Let dry.

Glue leaves and berries to top of rolling pin. Let dry. ❁

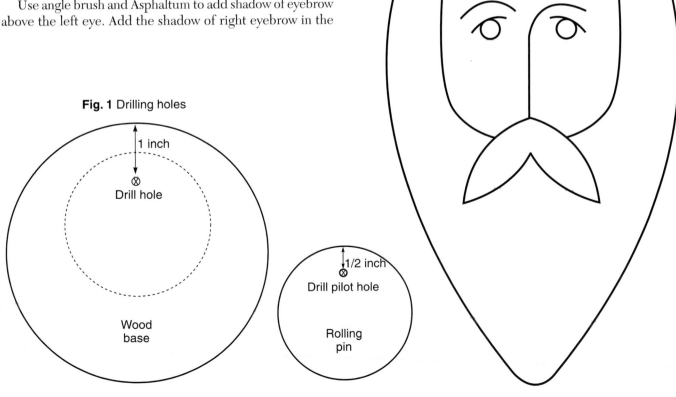

**SANTA FACE PATTERN**
Trace 1—tracing paper
Paint as directed

**Fig. 1** Drilling holes

1 inch
⊗ Drill hole

Wood base

1/2 inch
⊗ Drill pilot hole

Rolling pin

# Recipe Card Holder Has Seasonal Spice

*YOU'LL SWEETEN your baking when you use this wooden gingerbread girl from Brenda Whitney. The Harmony, Maine crafter attached a clothespin on back to hold a recipe card.*

**MATERIALS NEEDED:**
Patterns on next page
Tracing paper and pencil
Graphite paper
Dry ballpoint pen or stylus
18-inch length of 1 x 8 pine for gingerbread and base
3-inch x 5-inch piece of 1/4-inch-thick balsa wood for candy cane
1-1/2-inch x 2-inch piece of 1/8-inch-thick balsa wood for cookie sheet
Scroll or band saw
Drill with 1/8-inch bit
Sand paper
Tack cloth
Two 1-1/4-inch-long flat-head wood screws
Screwdriver
Brown wood stain and soft cloth

Paper towels
Water container
Foam plate or palette
Acrylic craft paints—black, burnt sienna, red, silver and white
Paintbrushes—No. 1 round, No. 2 flat, 3/4-inch flat and liner
Clear varnish and foam brush
Red plaid fabric—8-inch square for dress and 3/4-inch x 6-inch strip for bow
3-inch square of white solid fabric for apron
White all-purpose thread
Hand-sewing needle
40-inch length of white cotton yarn for hair
Spring-type clothespin
Wood glue
Scissors
Ruler

**FINISHED SIZE:** Recipe holder measures about 10 inches high x 8 inches wide.

**DIRECTIONS:**
**CUTTING:** Trace enlarged patterns onto tracing paper with pencil.

Place traced gingerbread girl and candy cane patterns on wood with grain lines matching as directed on patterns. Slip graphite paper between patterns and wood as directed. Use dry ballpoint pen or stylus to draw over pattern lines, transferring them onto wood.

Cut out gingerbread girl and candy cane wood pieces using scroll or band saw.

From 1 x 8 pine, cut a 3-inch-wide x 8-inch-long piece for base. Drill pilot holes through base where shown in Fig. 1 below right. Also drill a pilot hole into center of each gingerbread foot where shown on pattern.

Sand all wood pieces smooth. Wipe with tack cloth to remove sanding dust.

Screw base to bottom of gingerbread girl.

Glue clothespin vertically to the back of the head so that the clip end extends 1/2 inch above top of head. Let dry.

Using soft cloth, apply brown stain to entire base and gingerbread girl. Let dry.

**PAINTING:** Keep paper towels and water container handy to clean brushes. Place small dabs of each paint color onto foam plate or palette as needed. Add coats of paint as needed for complete coverage. Let paint dry after every application.

Refer to the photo above left as a guide while painting as directed in the instructions that follow.

**Gingerbread girl:** Place traced pattern on gingerbread girl with edges matching and slip graphite paper between pattern and wood. Use dry ballpoint pen or stylus to mark position of eyes, mouth and cheeks.

Dip end of liner handle into black and add dots for eyes.

Use round brush and black to add mouth.

Use round brush and white to paint cheeks. When dry, use round brush and red to add spirals to cheeks.

Thin white paint with clean water to an ink-like consistency. Use liner and thinned white to add wavy lines around outer edges on front of gingerbread.

**Candy Cane:** Use 3/4-inch flat brush and white to paint entire candy cane.

When dry, use No. 2 flat brush and liner to add wide and narrow red stripes to candy cane.

**Cookie sheet:** Paint 1-1/2- x 2-inch wood piece silver.

When dry, place cookie sheet pattern on top of silver wood piece. Slip graphite paper between pattern and wood. Trace

inside patterns with dry ballpoint pen or stylus, transferring four gingerbread cookie shapes onto cookie sheet.

Use No. 2 flat brush and burnt sienna to paint the gingerbread cookies.

When dry, use liner and black to add two tiny dots to each cookie for eyes.

**Finishing:** Use foam brush to apply varnish to all wood pieces. Let dry.

**HAIR AND BOW:** Cut about twenty 2-inch-long pieces of white cotton yarn for hair.

Stack yarn pieces in a bundle. Wrap plaid fabric strip around center of yarn bundle and tie ends in a knot.

**DRESS AND APRON:** Pull threads from all edges of plaid dress fabric piece and from white apron fabric piece to create fringe.

Center one edge of apron along one narrow edge of dress piece. Thread hand-sewing needle with white thread. Sew along top edge of dress and apron about 1/4 inch from edge with a running stitch. See Fig. 2 below for stitch illustration. Pull thread to gather edge to about 2 inches. Fasten off.

**ASSEMBLY:** Referring to photo for position, glue hair to top of head and glue dress to front of body.

Glue candy cane to front of upraised arm. Glue cookie sheet to top of other arm. Let dry. ❊

**RECIPE HOLDER PATTERNS**

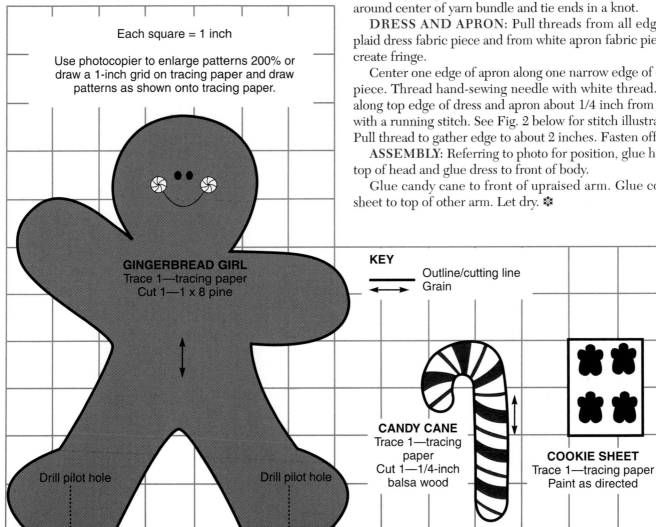

Each square = 1 inch

Use photocopier to enlarge patterns 200% or draw a 1-inch grid on tracing paper and draw patterns as shown onto tracing paper.

**GINGERBREAD GIRL**
Trace 1—tracing paper
Cut 1—1 x 8 pine

Drill pilot hole          Drill pilot hole

**KEY**
Outline/cutting line
Grain

**CANDY CANE**
Trace 1—tracing paper
Cut 1—1/4-inch balsa wood

**COOKIE SHEET**
Trace 1—tracing paper
Paint as directed

**Fig. 1** Drilling pilot holes through base

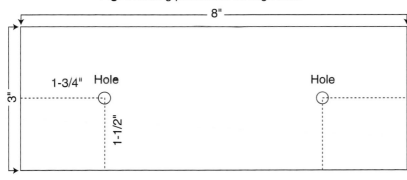

8"

3"

1-3/4"   Hole          Hole

1-1/2"

**Fig. 2** Running stitch

## Candle Set Brings A Beautiful Glow

*WITH THE LIGHT from these silvery candle holders, Christmas will shine even brighter. "They can be enjoyed throughout the winter season," says Sandy Rollinger of Apollo, Pennsylvania.*

**MATERIALS NEEDED** (for all):
Two 2-inch-high clear glass votive holders
One 6-inch-high clear glass vase
White tissue paper
1-inch sponge brush
Sparkle Mod Podge
Oven-bake clay (Sandy used Sculpey)—Whipped Cream
Scrolls & Swirls Texture Maker sheet (Sandy used Sculpey ST 1449)
Clay roller
Plastic mat
Craft knife
Patterns on this page
Tracing paper and pencil
Foil-lined baking sheet
Powdered pigment (Sandy used Jacquard Pearl-Ex Micro Pearl 650)
Small flat paintbrush
2-inch-wide silver-and-white ribbon to fit around vase
1-inch-wide silver-and-white ribbon to fit around vase and both votive holders
1/4-inch-wide silver ribbon to fit around votive holders
Two 1/2-inch rhinestone stars
One 1-inch rhinestone snowflake
Craft glue (Sandy used Beacon Adhesives Fabri-Tac and Gem-Tac)
Ruler
Scissors

**FINISHED SIZE:** Large candle holder measures about 6 inches high x 4 inches across. Each small candle holder measures about 2 inches high x 2 inches across.

**DIRECTIONS:**
Trace large and small star patterns onto tracing paper with pencil. Cut out patterns following outline of each.

Condition clay and roll it to a 1/8-inch thickness on plastic mat.

Place texture sheet on top of clay. Use clay roller to press pattern into clay. Remove texture sheet.

Place patterns on textured clay. Use craft knife to cut out one large star and two small stars following pattern outlines.

Place stars on foil-lined baking sheet. Bake following clay manufacturer's instructions. Let cool.

Use paintbrush to apply powdered pigment to front of stars. Let dry.

Tear white tissue paper into small pieces.

**LARGE CANDLE HOLDER:** Use sponge brush to apply Sparkle Mod Podge to a small area on outside of vase. Adhere tissue paper pieces to vase. Repeat to cover the entire outside of vase. Let dry.

Cut a length of 2-inch-wide ribbon and 1-inch-wide ribbon to fit around vase.

Apply Fabri-Tac around center of vase and adhere the 2-inch-wide ribbon piece around vase.

Apply Fabri-Tac around center of 2-inch-wide ribbon and adhere 1-inch-wide ribbon around vase, positioning all ribbon ends in the same place on vase. Let dry.

Use Gem-Tac to adhere rhinestone snowflake to center of large clay snowflake. Glue snowflake to ribbons, covering the ribbon ends. Let dry.

**SMALL CANDLE HOLDERS:** Follow directions for large candle holder, using 1-inch-wide and 1/4-inch-wide ribbons, small clay stars and rhinestone stars instead. ❈

**STAR CANDLE HOLDER PATTERNS**

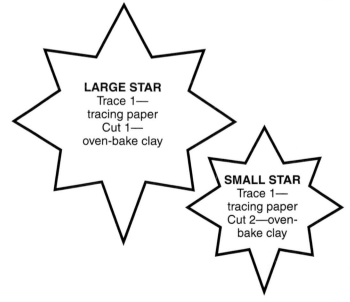

**LARGE STAR**
Trace 1—
tracing paper
Cut 1—
oven-bake clay

**SMALL STAR**
Trace 1—
tracing paper
Cut 2—oven-bake clay

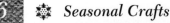

# Chase Chills with Snowy Knit Afghan

*WHAT BETTER WAY to warm up from winter than with an afghan patterned after snowflakes? Sue Childress of Judson, Texas knitted this cozy yet decorative blanket everyone will love.*

## MATERIALS NEEDED:
Off-white bulky yarn—nine 3.5 ounce/100-gram 103-yard skeins (Sue used Berroco-Peruvian Quick 100% Peruvian Highland Wool yarn in Blanco)
Size 11 (8mm) 29-inch circular needles (or size needed to obtain correct gauge)
Yarn or tapestry needle
Scissors

**GAUGE:** 12 sts and 16 rows = 4 inches.

## SPECIAL STITCH:
Inc = Increase: Pull up bar before next st, place on left needle, k this st.

**FINISHED SIZE:** Afghan measures about 44 inches square.

## DIRECTIONS:
Cast on 115 sts.

**Lattice Stitch Border: Row 1 (RS):** K 3, [p 1, k 5] across to last 4 sts, p 1, k 3: 115 sts.

**Row 2:** P 2, [k 1, p 1, k 1, p 3] across to last 5 sts, k 1, p 1, k 1, p 2: 115 sts.

**Row 3:** K 1, [p 1, k 3, p 1, k 1] across: 115 sts.

**Row 4:** K 1, [p 5, k 1] across: 115 sts.

**Row 5:** K 1, [p 1, k 3, p 1, k 1]: 115 sts.

**Row 6:** P 2 [k 1, p 1, k 1, p 3] across to last 5 sts, k 1, p 1, k 1, p 2: 115 sts.

Repeat Rows 1-6 twice.

Repeat Rows 1-5 once.

**Last Row:** P 2, k 1, p 1, k 1, p 3, k 1, p 1, k 1, p 2, inc, [k 1, p 1, k 1, p 3] across to last 13 sts (working p 2 in last repeat), inc, p 2, k 1, p 1, k 1, p 3, k 1, p 1, k 1, p 2: 117 sts.

**Center Section: Row 1:** K 3, p 1, k 5, p 1, k 4, [yo, sl 1, k 1, psso, k 1, k2tog, yo, k 1] across to last 13 sts, k 3, p 1, k 5, p 1, k 3: 117 sts.

**Row 2:** P 2, k 1, p 1, k 1, p 3, k 1, p 1, k 1, p across to last 11 sts, k 1, p 1, k 1, p 3, k 1, p 1, k 1, p 2: 117 sts.

**Row 3:** K 1, [p 1, k 3, p 1, k 1] twice, k 2, yo, [k 3, yo] across to last 15 sts, k 3, [p 1, k 3, p 1, k 1] twice: 147 sts.

**Row 4:** K 1, [p 5, k 1] twice, p across to last 13 sts, k 1 [p 5, k 1] twice: 147 sts.

**Row 5:** K 1, [p 1, k 3, p 1, k 1] twice, k2tog, yo, sl 1, k 1, psso, k 1, k2tog, yo, [sl 1, k2tog, psso, yo, sl 1, k 1, psso, k 1, k2tog, yo] across to last 15 sts, sl 1, k 1, psso, k 1, [p 1, k 3, p 1, k 1] twice: 117 sts.

**Row 6:** P 2, k 1, p 1, k 1, p 3, k 1, p 1, k 1, p across to last 11 sts, k 1, p 1, k 1, p 3, k 1, p 1, k 1, p 2: 117 sts.

**Row 7:** K 3, p 1, k 5, p 1, k 4, [k2tog, yo, k 1, yo, sl 1, k 1, psso, k 1] across to last 13 sts, k 3, p 1, k 5, p 1, k 3: 117 sts.

**Row 8:** P 2, k 1, p 1, k 1, p 3, k 1, p 1, k 1, p across to last 11 sts, k 1, p 1, k 1, p 3, k 1, p 1, k 1, p 2: 117 sts.

**Row 9:** K 1, [p 1, k 3, p 1, k 1] twice, k 2, yo, [k 3, yo] across to last 15 sts, k 3, [p 1, k 3, p 1, k 1] twice: 147 sts.

**Row 10:** K 1, [p 5, k 1] twice, p across to last 13 sts, k 1, [p 5, k 1] twice: 147 sts.

**Row 11:** K 1, [p 1, k 3, p 1, k 1] twice, k 1, [k2tog, yo, sl 1, k2tog, psso, yo, sl 1, k 1, psso, k 1] across to last 13 sts, k 1, [p 1, k 3, p 1, k 1] twice: 117 sts.

**Row 12:** P 2, k 1, p 1, k 1, p 3, k 1, p 1, k 1, p across to last 11 sts, k 1, p 1, k 1, p 3, k 1, p 1, k 1, p 2: 117 sts.

Repeat Rows 1-12 thirteen times or until piece measures about 36 inches, ending with Row 11: 117 sts.

**Last Row of Center Section:** P 2, k 1, p 1, k 1, p 3, k 1, p 1, k 1, p 2, p2tog, p across to last 15 sts, p2tog, p 2, k 1, p 1, k 1, p 3, k 1, p 1, k 1, p 2: 115 sts.

Repeat Rows 1-6 of Lattice Stitch Border three times.
Bind off loosely.

Weave in all loose ends with yarn or tapestry needle. ❁

# Make Outdoor Christmas Decorating
## Fun for the Family!

Outside trimming—a chore? Not when you bundle up the gang and turn it into a family affair of fresh-air activity, then a warm-up meal.

STRINGING LIGHTS on trees...hanging wreaths on the house...setting up illuminated figurines...decorating outside for Christmas can seem like just one more task on your holiday "to-do" list. But it doesn't have to be! Why not turn that project from drudgery into festivity by getting the whole family involved together?

Children will be proud to help, and you'll have extra time to spend as a family during the hectic holiday season. Give kids their own special "assignment"—decorating the yard with snow angels or a dressed-up snowman.

After the merrymaking outdoors, head back in the house for a hearty dinner of chili (made ahead in the slow cooker), hot chocolate, tree-shaped cutout cookies and other easy-to-fix treats (see the recipes on pages 110-111).

Your family may just find your "outdoor decorating day" to be a real blast—and ask to do it again next year!

# Zippy Beef Chili

~Bonnie Chocallo, Wyoming, Pennsylvania

2 pounds lean ground beef
1 can (16 ounces) kidney beans, rinsed and drained
2 cans (14-1/2 ounces *each*) diced tomatoes
1 can (11-1/2 ounces) pork and beans
2 large onions, chopped
2 medium carrots, shredded
1 medium sweet red pepper, chopped
1 medium green pepper, chopped
2 celery ribs, chopped
1 cup water
1/2 cup ketchup
1 can (6 ounces) tomato paste
2 jalapeno peppers, seeded and chopped
3 tablespoons brown sugar
4 garlic cloves, minced
1 tablespoon dried oregano
1 tablespoon chili powder
1 teaspoon salt
1 teaspoon crushed red pepper flakes
1 teaspoon pepper

In a large skillet, cook beef over medium heat until no longer pink; drain. Transfer to a 5-qt. slow cooker. Add remaining ingredients. Cover and cook on low for 6 hours. **Yield:** 12 servings.

**Editor's Note:** When cutting hot peppers, disposable gloves are recommended. Avoid touching your face.

# Christmas Tree Savory Rolls

~Maryalice Wood, Langley, British Columbia

4 to 4-1/2 cups all-purpose flour
2/3 cup sugar
1 tablespoon active dry yeast
2 teaspoons grated lemon peel
1 teaspoon salt
3/4 cup milk
2/3 cup water
1/3 cup canola oil
1 tablespoon lemon juice
FILLING:
1 package (8 ounces) cream cheese, softened, *divided*
2 tablespoons mayonnaise
2 teaspoons lemon juice, *divided*
1 teaspoon lemon-pepper seasoning
1 teaspoon dried parsley flakes
1 can (6 ounces) crabmeat, drained, flaked and cartilage removed, optional
1 *each* small green and sweet red pepper
1 medium lemon

**1.** In a large bowl, combine 3 cups flour, sugar, yeast, lemon peel and salt. In a small saucepan, heat milk and water to 120°-130°. Stir in oil and lemon juice. Add to dry ingredients; beat until smooth. Stir in enough remaining flour to form a soft dough. Turn onto a floured surface; knead until smooth and elastic, about 6-8 minutes. Place in a greased bowl, turning once to grease the top. Cover and let rise in a warm place until doubled, about 1 hour.

**2.** Meanwhile, in a small bowl, beat 4 ounces cream cheese until smooth. Add mayonnaise, 1 teaspoon lemon juice, seasoning and parsley; mix well. Stir in crab if desired; set aside.

**3.** Turn dough onto a lightly floured surface; roll out into a 22-in. x 14-in. rectangle. Spread prepared filling to within 1/2 in. of edges. Roll up jelly-roll style, starting with a long side; pinch seams to seal. Cut into 22 slices.

**4.** Cover a baking sheet with foil and grease well. Place one slice near the top center of prepared baking sheet. Place two slices in the second row with sides touching. Repeat, adding one slice per row, until tree has five rows. Repeat last row. Center remaining two slices below last row for trunk. Cover and let rise until doubled, about 30 minutes. Bake at 325°

for 25-30 minutes or until golden brown. Carefully transfer rolls with foil onto a wire rack to cool completely.

**5.** Meanwhile, in a small bowl, beat remaining cream cheese and lemon juice until smooth. Cut a small hole in the corner of pastry or plastic bag; fill with cream cheese mixture. Pipe onto rolls for garland.

**6.** Cut peppers in half vertically; remove stems and seeds. Using 1-1/2-in. and 2-in. star cookie cutters, cut stars from peppers; place on tree. Remove a 2-in. piece of peel from lemon (save lemon for another use). With 2-in. star cookie cutter, cut a star from peel; place on top of tree. Remove foil before serving. Refrigerate leftovers. **Yield:** 1 tree (22 rolls).

# White Chocolate Brandy Alexander

*~Sharon Delaney-Chronis, South Milwaukee, Wisconsin*

3-1/2 cups milk
  1/2 teaspoon vanilla extract
  1/8 teaspoon salt
    6 ounces white baking chocolate, finely chopped
  1/3 cup brandy
  1/4 cup creme de cacao
Whipped topping and white chocolate shavings, optional

In a large saucepan, heat milk, vanilla and salt over medium heat just until mixture comes to a simmer. Remove from heat. Add chocolate; whisk until mixture is smooth. Stir in brandy and creme de cacao. Fill mugs three-fourths full. Top with whipped cream and shavings if desired. **Yield:** 6 servings.

# Caramel Hot Chocolate

*~Maureen Mitchell, Calgary, Alberta*

  4 cups nonfat dry milk powder
  3/4 cup baking cocoa
  1/2 cup sugar
    8 cups water

    1 Caramello candy bar (2.7 ounces), chopped
Whipped cream and grated chocolate, optional

**1.** In a 3-qt. slow cooker, combine the milk powder, cocoa and sugar; gradually whisk in water until smooth. Cover and cook on low for 4 hours or until hot.

**2.** Add candy bar; stir until melted. Garnish with whipped cream and grated chocolate if desired. **Yield:** about 2 quarts.

# Christmas Tree Sugar Cookies

*~Janaan Cunningham, Greendale, Wisconsin*

    1 cup butter, softened
1-1/2 cups confectioners' sugar
    1 egg
    1 teaspoon vanilla extract
  1/2 teaspoon almond extract
2-1/2 cups all-purpose flour
    1 teaspoon baking soda
    1 teaspoon cream of tartar
  1/2 teaspoon salt
ICING:
    2 cups confectioners' sugar
    2 tablespoons plus 2 teaspoons milk
Green paste food coloring
Lightbulb-shaped sprinkles

**1.** In a large bowl, cream butter and confectioners' sugar. Beat in egg and extracts. Combine the flour, baking soda, cream of tartar and salt; gradually add to creamed mixture and mix well. Cover and refrigerate for 2 hours or until easy to handle.

**2.** On a lightly floured surface, roll out dough to 1/8-in. thickness. Cut with a floured 4-in. x 3-in. tree cookie cutter. Place 2 in. apart on greased baking sheets. Bake at 375° for 6-8 minutes or until lightly browned. Remove to wire racks to cool.

**3.** For icing, in a bowl, combine confectioners' sugar and milk. Remove 1/3 cup icing to a small bowl; tint dark green with food coloring. Tint remaining icing light green; spread over cookies. Cut a small hole in the corner of a pastry or plastic bag; fill bag with dark green icing. Pipe string for lights onto trees; add sprinkles for bulbs. **Yield:** about 1-1/2 dozen.

# A Season of Miracles

*Chance encounters…lucky coincidences…unexpected blessings…
read about these unforgettable events in the lives of country women.*

## Very "Claus" Call

I'LL NEVER FORGET the Christmas when the flu sidelined the gentleman who always visited our children as Santa Claus. My husband, George, and I were at a loss about how to explain the jolly elf's absence and asked a few friends for suggestions.

December 24 came, and we still hadn't come up with a story. Amazingly, that evening, the doorbell rang and in walked Santa. He'd recovered just in time! But what astounded us even more was what happened next.

Within half an hour, the doorbell rang again. It was a neighbor who'd heard of our dilemma and suited himself up as a Santa substitute. We welcomed him in; then a knock came at the back door. You guessed it—*another* St. Nick, a third thoughtful friend.

The kids were thrilled to have been visited by Santa and two of his helpers that Christmas Eve. And George and I were deeply touched to realize what wonderful people there are in this world.

~*Evelyn Falk, Hales Corners, Wisconsin*

## Deer-est Friends

I WAS ALONE at home and knew something was terribly wrong. A former nurse, I tried to remain calm and take stock of the physical symptoms I was experiencing. And I realized there was only one explanation—I had suffered a stroke.

My legs seemed to be functioning better than my arms, and I urged my numb limbs to carry me out to the road that ran past my house. When I got outside, I saw a cluster of deer that I'd been feeding regularly all winter.

Seeing a truck approaching, I tried to wave. But the truck sped past me, oblivious to my emergency. I felt my fear building…and those deer must have sensed my helplessness.

In unison, they walked out to the middle of the road and stopped. They stood there, unmoving, even as another big truck thundered toward them. When the driver was forced to slow down, he saw me and realized something was wrong. He quickly came to my aid and got me to the hospital.

After rehabilitation, I'm stronger now than ever—thanks not only to my determination, but also to my angels, the deer.

~*Patrice Vacca, Moscow, Pennsylvania*

## A Warm Glow

AFTER a massive ice storm left us without power—or heat—for 8 days, I knew I should get a wood-burning insert for our inefficient fireplace so we wouldn't go through that situation again. But I couldn't afford the nearly $3,000 cost. I said a little prayer to God as I kept my eye out for a used one.

The very next day, something told me to stop at the country store to check its bulletin board. I saw a flyer for a used insert, just 2 miles from my house, for only $100.

The owner had planned to take the ad down the previous day, she said, but felt compelled to leave it up a few more days. I was thrilled that it was exactly the right size—but worried about how I'd get it home without a truck.

The woman's husband then offered to deliver it if my sons would just lend a hand. At that point, I was so thankful that I hugged a couple of strangers!

And when the next power outage hit, our house stayed warm.

~*Barb Marshall, Canal Winchester, Ohio*

## Gift from an Angel

MY HUSBAND had recently passed away after months in the hospital, and the money I'd saved for Christmas was almost totally gone. It had been used to pay caregivers to stay at his bedside when I couldn't be there.

I stayed with him each day from 8 p.m. to 2 a.m., then drove home, caught a few hours of sleep and went next door to help my mom, who was also in poor health. Getting a job was nearly impossible until I could find someone to stay with her, and the small income I did have was barely enough to cover monthly expenses.

Then came the final blow. I received a large credit card bill, listing charges from a trip taken before my husband's illness had become terminal. I tossed and turned every night, wondering how I was ever going to pay that sum of money.

Just before the date the credit card payment was due, I was sorting through my mail and found a peculiar envelope. When I opened it, there was a letter informing me that one of my father's relatives (of whom I never knew) had passed away in another state and included me in his will.

Enclosed with the letter was a check. It was made out, almost to the penny, for the amount of my debt.

Whenever I look back on this challenging time in my life, I think of the words from one of my devotional books. "Because God never sleeps, we can sleep in peace."

~*Mary Turner, Blountville, Tennessee*

## One Shining Moment

OUR SON was 6 when he was diagnosed with juvenile diabetes. He would need carefully timed doses of insulin. After a week in the hospital, he was finally allowed to come home. On that same day, a northeaster blew in, full force.

Reluctantly, my husband left me with our son and headed off to his night job. I nervously prepared to give our little boy his very first insulin injection as the storm raged outside.

Smilingly reassuringly, I called him to me and picked up the syringe. At that moment, a gust of wind howled, and the lights flickered, dimmed and died.

In total darkness, I fought back a wave of panic. Suddenly, the lights blinked back on. I quickly administered the shot, and just as I finished and kissed our son, the lights went out again.

The power stayed off well into the next day, but I could hardly be upset. The Lord had shone His light on us exactly when we needed it most.

~*Susan True, Hampden, Maine*

# Recipe and Craft Index